A YEAR IN
FOOD AND BEER

AltaMira Studies in Food and Gastronomy

General Editor: Ken Albala, Professor of History, University of the Pacific (kalbala@pacific.edu)
AltaMira Executive Editor: Wendi Schnaufer (wschnaufer@rowman.com)

Food Studies is a vibrant and thriving field encompassing not only cooking and eating habits but issues such as health, sustainability, food safety, and animal rights. Scholars in disciplines as diverse as history, anthropology, sociology, literature, and the arts focus on food. The mission of **AltaMira Studies in Food and Gastronomy** is to publish the best in food scholarship, harnessing the energy, ideas, and creativity of a wide array of food writers today. This broad line of food-related titles will range from food history, interdisciplinary food studies monographs, general interest series, and popular trade titles to textbooks for students and budding chefs, scholarly cookbooks, and reference works.

A YEAR IN FOOD AND BEER

RECIPES and BEER PAIRINGS for EVERY SEASON

EMILY BAIME and DARIN MICHAELS

A division of
ROWMAN & LITTLEFIELD PUBLISHERS, INC.
Lanham • New York • Toronto • Plymouth, UK

Published by AltaMira Press
A division of Rowman & Littlefield Publishers, Inc.
A wholly owned subsidiary of The Rowman & Littlefield Publishing Group, Inc.
4501 Forbes Boulevard, Suite 200, Lanham, Maryland 20706
www.rowman.com

10 Thornbury Road, Plymouth PL6 7PP, United Kingdom

British Library Cataloguing in Publication Information Available

Library of Congress Cataloging-in-Publication Data
Baime, Emily.
  A year in food and beer : recipes and beer pairings for every season / Emily Baime and
Darin Michaels.
     pages cm
  Includes bibliographical references and index.
  ISBN 978-0-7591-2263-5 (cloth : alkaline paper) —   ISBN 978-0-7591-2265-9 (ebook)
  1. Cooking, American. 2. Food and beer pairing. 3. Seasonal cooking. I. Michaels,
Darin. II. Title.
  TX715.B1616 2013
  641.5973—dc23
                                                                          2013001922

Printed in the United States of America

To our families and the beer bellies

Contents

Preface

Emily and Darin met through beer: Darin as the beer sales representative, Emily as the community events organizer. Together they have created Community Tap and Table, hands-on cooking classes, personal chef services, culinary travel and beer-wine-food pairing expertise. This book contains recipes and beer pairings tested on several hundred "beer bellies" at these cooking activities. The goal of *A Year in Food and Beer* is to bring the same passion for great beer, great food, and entertaining from Community Tap and Table into your kitchen.

Emily has a passion for food exploration, Darin for beer and brewing. As their passion developed together into a focus on pairing, they found a void in the culinary landscape: quality beer and food pairing education. Living in California's Central Valley, they have at their doorstep northern California's craft beer revolution, San Francisco's dynamic food scene and brewing and viticulture education at local universities and are surrounded by rich agricultural production. This book weaves these influences together.

While they enjoy the adventurous attempts of beer bars and breweries to provide quality food, many offer only repetitive and mainstream foods. On the flip side, quality restaurants offer seasonal, inventive cuisine but only with wine pairing, with less than a slight nod toward beer. This book bridges these foods with craft brews. The authors believe that just as wine flavors vary within varietal, and vary even from year to year from the same vineyards, so do beer flavors and varieties. Their recipes and menus are created after detailed tasting of a single brew, designed to highlight the smallest detail within the beer.

Emily was raised in San Diego, Darin in Seattle. Recipes and brews in this book span the Mexican influence of Southern California to the fresh seafoods of Washington State. The beers span the United States. Many excellent brews have been omitted, not from their table but from this book, in an effort to offer recipes that teach diverse food preparation.

Cheers!

CHAPTER 1

Artfully Pairing Food and Beer

Food and beer pairing is as much an art form as pairing food with wine, but it has yet to be as fully explored. The goal of this book is to educate the reader on the depths of flavors found in artfully paired gourmet foods and craft beer.

A Year in Food and Beer develops the reader's expertise in identifying flavors in beers, linking those flavors to seasonal, gourmet foods. Rather than assume all "beer-friendly" food must be heavy, greasy, and reeking of entrails, we believe in crafting gourmet, seasonal foods designed for communal eating experiences and entertaining. Here, more than forty recipes and brews have been carefully selected to build both culinary knowledge and an understanding of the many flavorful styles of beer. The reader will be exposed to gourmet culinary techniques to create meals that pair with the most prevalent American craft beers including American versions of trendy European beers as well as offbeat Belgian and German beers.

In this chapter the reader can develop a base of knowledge before turning to selecting a seasonal party menu, beer type, cooking technique, ingredient, or specific brew. Note that although the recipes and pairings ensure the home cook's success in reproducing the food and beer pairing experience exactly, the purpose of this book is not to promote one specific recipe, beer, or brewery. Rather it is to encourage the readers to begin their own beer-food pairing journey. Each chapter identifies characteristics in the recommended beers such as predominant flavors, bitterness units, alcohol content, and brewing style and explains why these beers pair with a specific technique in food preparation such as smoking, preserving, curing, roasting, broiling, and pickling. The pairing of food flavors and culinary techniques within beer styles can then be applied to the recommended beers and specific recipes. This will also build a food-beer pairing tool kit for readers to apply pairing skills to other recipes or favorite brews.

Beer: A Seasonal Symphony

We believe there is a natural link when comparing beer and classical music. To perfect the music performed, the members of the orchestra must work in perfect technical precision. Their dedication to the science of their craft becomes almost unnoticeable if the music is performed correctly. The science manifests itself as a seamless artistic performance. The brewing process is the same.

As the brewers orchestrate the presence of sweet malts, pungent hops, alcohol, and stinging or smooth effervescence, their technical precision manifests itself as perfection in a bottle. The hours of yeast analysis and brew kettle oversight synthesize into a liquid art. This art can be heightened by proper culinary pairings.

In each seasonal chapter of this book, the brews discussed are likened to different sounds found in a symphony. The goal of each chapter is to bring these dominant seasonal sounds (flavors) into concert with the recipes. The reader is the conductor of this experience.

Spring represents the high, flirty trills of a symphony. These brews tend toward bold yet light, stinging and slightly sour flavors. Summer represents the celebratory, high-energy percussion drums of a symphony. They tend toward citric, hopped, fruit-forward, and in-your-face flavors. Fall represents the sexy, sultry saxophones. They tend toward caramel, coating, and rich flavors. Winter represents the slow booming drums and lonely piano solos of a symphony. They tend toward dark, heavy roasted flavors and thicker, syrupy textures.

Exploring Flavors in Food and Beer

All five senses should be used to enjoy the ambiance of a food-beer pairing. One should strive to become aware of the sights, sounds, flavors, smells, and textures of food and beer before attempting to pair them. Mindful eating and drinking helps identify familiar flavors and encourages exploration of new flavors.

Create a list of familiar foods that you enjoy often. For example, is pasta a regular staple? What sauces are usually involved? Tomato based or cream? Add notes to the familiar foods regarding regular flavors and textures. For example, is the tomato sauce acidic and sweet with herbs and spice? Is the cream sauce rich, tongue coating, and smooth? Another example is chicken or beef a regular staple? What condiments are used with these proteins? Sweet, thick catsup or savory teraki? Review lists of seasonal produce and add those to the list. For example, are sweet yellow squash and watermelon on the table often in summer? Are kale and lettuce part of your regular winter diet? Are asparagus and radishes a spring staple? Now expand the list with future food exploration. Revisit a list of seasonal produce and add a few that have not been explored. For example, what pasta sauces would be interesting to explore and how can more flavors be incorporated? Is a herb heavy, burnt butter sauce appealing, or a root vegetable sauce with fiery-hot seafood? In the spring, would you prefer flower blossoms join the pasta, or in the fall does fatty pork belly and pomegranate cross the pasta plate? If not, would you like them to? No answer is incorrect. The purpose of the exercise is to notice your current eating habits and enhance them with new experiences and deeper flavor exploration to whet the appetite for adventure.

As a beer is poured or an ingredient selected, a visceral experience should take place. Notice the color and texture of the brew and work to recall where those colors and textures are found in food. Lots of bubbles and a straw color reminds us of pink shrimp. Midnight-black, thick brews remind us of thick Irish stews. Inhale the fragrance above a beer glass as the beer is poured and smell dried spices from the spice rack until the nose matches a flavor in both the beer and the spice. Consider that spice. In what genre of food is that spice found? For example, for a bright pilsner, smelling the brew and spices might link white pepper, nutmeg, fresh-cut grass, and apple, all flavors found in the fall, on a pork roast, at the holiday table, and in Indian and French cooking. As another example, pour a deep porter. On the nose, notice coffee, chocolate, burnt toast, and lavender. This may link to grilled summer red meats and slow-roasted winter red meats with sweet vegetables. Pour an Irish Red. On the nose, notice caramel, butter biscuits, and sweet eggplant. This may link to cheddary fondue, bacon, or smokey sauce. Again, no reference is incorrect; flavor linkages depend on the individual experience and palate. The purpose of the exercise is to awaken the sensory organs and to invite exploration.

Notice the sound of cooking. Is the food raw and hearty, making tearing or chopping sounds like cutting a lettuce? Does the food sizzle as it settles into hot oil like fried potatoes? Is the food silent, roasting slowly or spreading softly? What texture does the food hold? Hard, dense, and cold like a raw carrot, silky like seafood, or airy and light like whipped cream? A smooth, creamy texture may be enlivened by a high-effervescent brew or may become decadent with a smooth, creamy stout. A cold, dense texture could be balanced by a spicy India Pale Ale (IPA) or accentuated by a crisp lager. Sizzling cooking sounds usually mean the integration of oils, butters, and other fats into the food, inviting the pairing of highly hopped brews to power through oil on the tongue.

Exploring flavors in the food that already grace the palate will help develop a natural tendency for successful pairings. If spicy, grilled flavors are preferred, the Summer chapter has the pairings to explore first. If tart, tangy, and bright flavors are preferred, the Spring chapter may have the pairings to explore. If bold, sweet, and roasty flavors are preferred, the Winter chapter may have the pairings to review first. If fatty, yeasty flavors are preferred, the Fall chapter is a good starting point.

4

Hands-on Exercise

To structure the exploration of visual appearance, sound, fragrance, texture, and flavor of food and beers, consider participating in this specific exercise. Visit a high-quality grocery, bottle shop, or brew pub and select four brews not previously tasted. Pick on a whim anything that appears interesting that you have not had before or have little exposure to. Chill the beers to 40 degrees before opening. Pour them into four glasses. A discussion on temperature, pouring technique, and glassware follows, but never mind that for now. On a sheet of paper, write down the color of each, omitting the terms red, yellow, brown, or black. Suggested colors may be auburn, golden, straw, amber, ruby, onyx, or any others that emerge.

Next, open five to ten dried spices or sauces from the cabinet. These might be salt, pepper, parsley, cinnamon, chocolate, oregano, barbeque sauce, and vanilla. Again, these are just suggestions. Smell the first brew just once, then smell a few spices. Are they similar flavors or do they contrast? Do you enjoy the combination or is it off-putting? Smell the brew again and see whether it smells differently now after smelling the spices. Continue this for all four brews and make a note of what each brew smells like. Some may have a few things to note after each spice, some may only have one. Suggested smells may be burnt, wheat, herbal, citrus, nutty, grassy, chocolate, or any others that emerge.

Now taste the brews. Snack on a plain cracker or mild bread between brews to refresh the tongue. Refrain from assigning a like or dislike label to any brew. Instead name the flavors in the brew and write down whether those flavors are familiar or unfamiliar. Does a Saison taste of flowers or Parmesan or maybe even a bit like a wet stable? Does an IPA taste of rosemary or citrus or maybe even taste like sticky dandelion? Does a cider taste of fruit and cheddar or maybe even taste too sweet? Does a Brown taste of hazelnuts or raspberries or maybe overly syrupy? Does a Pilsner taste of popcorn or bread or maybe watery? Does a barleywine taste of raisins or vanilla or maybe pungent blue cheese?

Bring the exercise to a close by reviewing the notes of familiar foods compared with the notes about the four brews explored. Most likely themes will arise between the familiar foods and the brews enjoyed. Sweet, meaty, and roasty point to the Winter chapter of this book; sour, light, and bright are found in the Spring chapter; juicy, fruity, and spicy are found in the Summer chapter; fatty, salty, and yeasty are found in the Fall chapter.

Why Seasonality Matters

Today, the benefits of organic food production, local eating, and the import/export of foods are under constant discussion. Eating produce while it is in season means that it will be fresher and more flavorful. Eating flavorful produce will highlight more complex flavors in paired brews.

In the Slow Food Movement, which values the good, clean, and fair treatment of our food system, respect for suppliers, seasonality, and local food production come first. Even outside this movement, chefs and foodies pursue fresh, flavorful, organic foods to enhance the flavors in their dishes. Organic food protects humans by harvesting and growing food by exposing them to fewer or safer chemicals. The same is true for those eating organic food. A laboratory is not needed to determine that fresh food also has more flavors. Food is fresher if it is eaten at harvest time rather than after long-distance travel. Food can be picked when ripe if it is grown locally. Food that travels is harvested when underripe to prevent rotting during travel, which increases the flavor. Foods that are eaten or preserved while fresh and in season will offer more complexity in beer pairing. Beer is a perishable item and, except for a beer that is bottle conditioned, offers better flavor when freshly brewed.

To source the quality ingredients discussed in this book, develop great relationships with local farmers, butchers, bottle shop owners, brewers, and cheesemongers. These relationships should not be "transactional," based on what is listed in the sale flyer and structured around getting "a good deal." These relationships should grow into friendships, based on a shared passion for great products. Express a passion for quality and adventure to these food professionals. Ask their opinion about cuts of meat and how to prepare them. Buy the new beer that they recommend. Ask to join them the next time the cheese supplier calls on them with samples. Refer friends to support their business. Because the money flows from consumer to retailer to producer, there is a misconception that the retailer works for the consumer. How can that be when it is the expert taste buds of the retailer and skills of the producer that determine exactly what product is even available to consumers? Our entire food system is at the mercy of those who grow and sell these products. If breweries do not protect their yeast strains from batch to batch, no amount of "the customer is always right" temper tantrum will produce a specific treasured beer; it is gone forever. The same is true of original seed strains used on family farms, recipes shared between generations in family restaurants, and cheese-making methods on organic dairies. Develop friendships with these expert suppliers to build a gourmet pantry and cellar. Support their craft so they can support your epicurean adventure.

Selecting Ingredients

Selecting a flavorful protein from the land (beef, chicken, lamb, or pork) requires three steps. First, the animal should have been raised on a pasture rather than in a cage. This means they were able to free feed and build more flavorful muscles rather than eat cheap feed quickly and build fat. Look for "free-range" and "cage-free" in the description. Second, the animals should have received minimal antibiotics. This means that they were not kept in such tight quarters that they needed repeat dosages of antibiotics and hence will not pass on antibiotics to you when you eat them. Ask the butcher or farmer to confirm that for you. Third, the meat should be as fresh as possible with bones included. The less the meat has been handled and cut down the more tender it will taste. The best way to ensure freshness is to buy large servings that have not been chopped and stored. For example, purchase the whole chicken or a side of beef, lamb, or pork. The butcher or farmer can cut the large animal part into smaller pieces for you right before you cook it. When you purchase proteins that have been processed and stored under light in plastic and Styrofoam, the meat begins to age and lose flavor.

Selecting these quality proteins that have been allowed to free graze and add weight slowly, rather than live in a pen and gain weight quickly, is important because the calcium and marrow from their bones provide flavor to the dish. Bone marrow, gelatins, calcium, and other minerals leave the bones and infuse the dishes. If the animal received antibiotics, did not receive proper nutrition, and was unable to exercise, the properties released will be unhealthy, just like the animal. If the animal is a flavorful breed that was not fed parts of other animals, was able to roam and breed naturally, and did not die in a stressful condition, the nutrient-rich properties will pass a rich, silky, and aromatic flavor and nutrients on to you.

When selecting a protein from the water, look for three items to ensure that the fish is fresh. When fish is fresh, it does not taste or smell "fishy"; it tastes sweet and meaty. First, the eyes of the fish should be brightly colored with clear white sections. Second, the scales should have a reflective shine and slick feel but should not be slimy. Third, the fish should smell of salt if from the ocean and moss if from the river but never fishy. If seafood sustainability is relevant to you, pick a breed of fish to eat using the Monterey Bay Aquarium's Seafood Watch List, available on their website.

Olive oil selection is the key to a strong cooking foundation. Most olive oil that sits in the grocery store, in clear or green glass bottles, imported from across an ocean, is stale by the time it is purchased. Clear and green bottles do not protect their contents from light or heat, both of which eventually make oil rancid and beer skunky. Buy local and use the oil quickly. Store both oil and beer in a cool, dark place.

Select the oil based on intended use. Is this oil to sauté with? "Sauté" means that a low to moderate heat will be applied to a flat, large pan and food will be cooked at this heat until done. Then select virgin oil. Cold-pressed, extra-virgin is no longer worth the extra cost as the oil will be heated and the flavor of the oil will shift to carry the food you are sautéing. Is the oil to fry or deep fry with? "Deep fry" means that the food being cooked is almost if not completely submerged in oil and cooked at a very high heat until fried. If this is the method of cooking, do not use cold pressed oil, just extra virgin. A large amount of oil is needed to fry and is very expensive. Various other oils can go to differing levels of heat before they reach what is called their smoke point or the highest heat they can achieve without burning. Olive oil has a very low smoke point compared with other oils. If the oil will be used to drizzle on salads or vegetables or added to sauces, use high-quality extra-virgin for flavor and health benefits.

To select dairy products, choose organic to ensure that the cow has regular access to pasture and has not been overly treated with antibiotics or growth hormones. This ensures that the flavor of the cow's food will shine through in the dairy. For example, cows from moist areas of northern California produce butters that are grassy and pale while cows from Wisconsin produce butters that are yellow and custardy. Many dairy cows are hooked up to milking machines for several hours per day, artificially impregnated annually to continue producing milk, and disposed of after only a few years. Selecting quality cream and milk is a simple way to participate in the more ethical treatment of production animals.

Care of Beer and Glassware

There are four major enemies of beer: light, heat, age, and air. Beer is perishable like milk and shares many of the same ingredients as bread. Neither milk nor bread would be best stored in heat or in sunlight or allowed to decay while exposed to the elements. Beer is protected from light by brown bottles or cans, from air by caps or corks, and from heat and age by those who ship and store it. Beer should be purchased chilled or at room temperature and stored between 35 and 45 degrees, depending on the beer style. It should not be stored in the trunk of a car or a hot garage or heated and cooled repeatedly. Higher-quality brewers will avoid clear or green bottles as clear allows light in and green actually amplifies ultraviolet light and speedy decay. Cans and brown glass are preferred. Cans and corks provide the most protection from air, followed closely by caps that require a bottle opener to open. Twist-top caps are more susceptible to slight air leaks that oxidize the beer. Craft brewers are turning toward can storage in increasing numbers because current aluminum technology provides an almost airtight seal and does not conduct heat to the level glass may. Beer is meant to be drunk as fresh as possible with the exception of beers that are bottle or cask conditioned with a cork. In the next chapter on brewing flavors we discuss brewing and bottle conditioning.

Each beer style has an ideal glass. Many beer-centric cultures (Germany, Belgium) offer a specific glass not just per style but for each individual beer within that style, changing with each glass of beer, each style of beer, and each annual batch. Brews that are highly effervescent like Pilsner and Lambic are best enjoyed in a cylinder or flute-style glass. This shape allows the bubbles to rise to the top and the light flavor of the brew to escape with each sip, similar to champagne. Brews that are light or low must benefit from a scored interior base that generates bubbles and maintains the lacy beer head. Floral, sour, or pungent brews are a fit for tulip-shaped glasses. This regulates the escape of strong smells and preserves the lesser amount of effervescence. Brews that are bold, roasty, and hoppy are served in a pint glass or mug to allow for large pours and because the bold flavors need no protection or guidance out of the glass. Higher-alcohol brews that are more viscous and syrupy benefit from a smaller pour in a snifter or red wine glass to allow the warmth of the beer to develop in the drinker's hand. If an arsenal of glassware is not realistic for your budget, storage, or interest levels, a pint glass and tulip glass will suffice. Next would come a snifter or red wine glass, than a flute.

Rivaling shape, cleanliness is the most important aspect of the glass. The brewing industry uses the phrase "beer clean," meaning that the glass is grease-free, will hold head, and leaves a lacy pattern of foam called Scottish Belgian Lace on the side of the interior of the glass as the beer recedes. Grease and soap on glassware will flatten the head and flavor of the brew. Clean your glassware in a grease-free dishwasher with petroleum-free dish soap or by hand with a clean sponge and unscented dish soap. Allow to dry upright as opposed to down on a towel where moisture can build up inside. To test the cleanliness of glassware, wet the inside of a glass and sprinkle it with table salt. The areas where the salt doesn't stick you have grease.

Storing and Serving Temperature

Store and serve brews at the temperature that best showcases their flavors. Lagers and wheat beers will be most refreshing and flavor forward at 35 to 45 degrees. Ales open up between 45 and 50 degrees. High-alcohol brews can be tempered by serving at 45 degrees or fully explored closer to 55 degrees.

Pouring

To pour a beer, tip the glass to a 45-degree angle, let the beer contact about halfway down, and fill the glass about a third of the way. Most importantly, do not allow the head of the beer or glass to touch the faucet or bottle to prevent the spread of flavor-killing bacteria. Still pouring, bring the beer back to 90 degrees and pour straight into the glass to develop the head and flavor of the beer. Obviously, individual brews benefit from specific pouring techniques, which are referenced as relevant in later chapters. Most importantly, do not allow the head of the beer to touch the faucet or bottle to prevent the spread of flavor-killing bacteria. Do not avoid creating head. A large percent of beer head, the foam that sits atop the beer, is beer. A sign of a well-brewed beer is a frothy head that is retained during the duration of drinking the beer. Lack of head indicates a flat brew, or unclean glassware, which should be avoided.

Tasting and pouring beer follow a similar method to wine tasting. Pour the beer into the glass, swirl it around, and notice the characteristics: color, carbonation, effervescence, viscosity, clarity, and head. Hold the glass close to the face to minimize distractions and mindfully focus on the beer. Smell the beer with closed eyes to again focus and identify the smells offered. Take a small sip of beer and swallow it. Flavor is tasted all the way down the throat. Notice the mouthfeel in terms of light, medium, or heavy. As food pairing enters the mix, immediately try a bite of the food and take another mouthful of beer. In our beer-food pairing classes, we repeat, "If you're chewing, you're drinking" to beer-food pairing attendees, the point being that, to experience the flavors together, they must both be in the mouth and on the tongue at least once, at exactly the same time.

To increase the flavor vocabulary and identify flavors in beer, research the Meilgaard Beer Flavor Wheel, found online under many sources. It is a visual diagram of flavors found in beer and is accepted by most in the brewing industry as the standard vocabulary. As beer is sipped, reference the flavors on the wheel and train your taste buds to identify flavors outside the usual sweet, salty, savory, sour, and umami such as nutty, grainy, grassy, citric, phenolic, stale, roasty, bitter, briny, and more. Epicureans who have entered the beer tasting arena will find this vocabulary translates back to food, and, all of a sudden, simple cereal becomes grainy, biscuity, and toasty floating in milk that is sweet, lactic, and slightly ripe.

How to Pair Food and Beer

Food and beer pairing starts first with identifying flavors in both the food and the beer, second comes the culinary techniques to link those flavors and finishes with the artful offering of complementary and contrasting flavors.

Those who are familiar with forms of color or food design will appreciate the concept of complementary or contrasting elements. Those who design with color may recognize this concept as using colors right next to each other in the spectrum to be complementary, such as orange and yellow, versus using colors from opposite ends of the spectrum to be contrasting, such as orange and blue. They may recognize the true skill in building a balanced room with orange, yellow, and blue. A simple example of complementary flavors in food would be beets and honey; both are sweet. A simple example of contrasting flavors in food would be peanut butter and jelly; one is salty and crunchy, one is sweet and smooth, but together they work. True artistry emerges when complementary and contrasting pairings emerge with a recipe. An example is beets roasted in complementary honey served with a contrasting salty crunch of crushed pistachios on a bed of bitter beet greens contrasted with floral lavender.

A natural assumption is that a certain style of food will always pair in a complementary or contrasting way with a certain type of brew. For example, many beer pairing dinners offer a Pilsner paired with a salad. Pilsners are likely to complement salads but only if the greens and proteins contained are mild, if no ripe tomatoes are present, and the dressing is light in dairy. A salad of broiled chicken, green apples, pine nuts, butter lettuce, and avocado with champagne vinaigrette would pair with most Pilsners but a salad of arugula, flank steak, candied pecans, blue cheese, and cranberry dressing would not. It would be better suited to a cranberry Lambic or a mild IPA. Barleywine is likely to complement chocolate if it is a sugary dessert but not a chocolate mole sauce. Despite the brew's chocolate flavor, the high alcohol pairs with sugar, not spice. A dry stout is much more likely to balance the dish.

It is also often assumed that certain culinary techniques will always lead to a pairing with certain brews. For example, the fried foods category can contain fried green tomatoes, fried pickles, or fried sweet breads. Categorically, fried foods do not automatically pair with a certain beer type or with "beer" generally. For example, the fried green tomato could be breaded in panko and dipped in a mayonnaise sauce, linking it to a light pale ale or bold Pilsner, or breaded in tempura and dipped in sesame sauce, linking it to a roasty red ale. Each dish within a food preparation category is changed depending on the sauces, fats, and spices. Each of the fried foods listed above could contain citric, sour, buttery, vinegar, or fatty flavors, leading to different beer pairings.

For success in pairing, link flavors rather than culinary techniques or genres of food. Referring back to the beer wheel, complementary flavors that are neighbors on the flavor wheel such as grassy or citrus pair well, and contrasting flavors across from one another on the wheel such as citrus and burnt pair well. Examples would be an orange chicken paired with a grassy pale ale through the use of green onions or an orange chicken paired with a roasty porter by adding a splash of spice. Artistry emerges when complementary and contrasting pairings are linked in one dish.

In this book we approach pairing beer and food as an art, not a science. To demonstrate this art, we offer more than one hundred examples of food flavors paired with brews contained in the seasonal and beer-cheese pairing chapters. Chapter 2 addresses how flavors develop in brews during the brewing process. This knowledge will help you in identifying flavors in beers before pairing with specific foods.

CHAPTER 2

Brewing Flavors

In this chapter we discuss how each step of the brewing process imparts flavor into the final product. We begin by linking brews to certain food flavors or culinary techniques. Instead of discussing beer fermentation from a scientist's approach, monitoring yeast activity in detail with microscopes and thermometers, we discuss how flavors enter beer in the brewing process. For example, a warmer open fermentation during a wet season can impart an almost haylike flavor in beer, linking it to ripe, soft cheeses and sour flavors. As a contrasting example, a closed colder fermentation imparts a cleaner, crisper flavor, linking those beers to dry, hard cheeses and tart flavors.

In the German style of brewing, beer has four basic ingredients: water, yeast, malt, and hops. Despite mass-marketing messaging, most water can be used to produce quality brew after pH balancing and the addition or removal of trace minerals. Yeast is the strain of live culture that converts sugar to alcohol and creates a by-product called CO_2 or carbonation. Basic brewing science involves soaking or "malting" the grain in water. These can include wheat, barley, or rye. Color develops in the brew based on the level of toasting that the grain has received before it enters the water. Darker malts have been heavily toasted and lead to a darker brew; lighter malts are untoasted or lightly toasted and lead to a lighter brew. Next, the water is boiled, which creates a sweet liquid called wort. Hops are then added to the boil to add flavoring. Hops are the flavoring agents, or "salt and pepper," of beer and add flavors of pine, citrus, and wood to the sweet brew. Then the batch is cooled and fermented with yeast to develop alcohol and bubbles.

In the American and Belgian-style brewing, these four ingredients are influenced by the addition of flavoring agents such as fruit, berries, wood, food, and spices. The two overarching options for fermentation are cold fermentation or warm fermentation. Cold, which brews lagers, means that the yeast ferments at the base of the brewing vessel. Warmer, which brews ales, means that the yeast ferments at the top. Open means that the beer ages uncovered in the fermentation tank, allowing wild yeast to combine with the beer yeast, imparting the flavors of the environment in which it was brewed. Closed means that the beer ages under the protection of the fermentation tank's lid, restricting the flavors to the yeast strain added by the brewer to the brew. To complicate matters, fermentation can take place in a tank, wooden barrel, or another container to add flavoring. There are two overarching types of brews: ales and lagers. Lagers are brewed at colder temperatures, are designed to be stored for much longer periods of time, and produce crisper flavors. Ales are brewed at warmer temperatures, are brewed to drink while fresh, and produce fruitier flavors. Entire libraries exist on the proper brewing process. The purpose of this discussion is to identify how differences in the brewing process create different beer flavors.

Within each category below are multiple subcategories and for every rule there is an exception. The following list is created to build a foundation for beer-food pairing knowledge and is not intended to be a bible on beer styles. Note that the specific beer categories listed follow those listed in Chapter 7.

- Pilsner: Expect light, crisp, hopped flavors and high effervescence because this lager is brewed at colder temperatures, cold fermented, medium hopped, filtered, and then stored to temper the hops. Pair with foods that benefit from bright, mildly citric, and lightly oiled flavors.
- Blonde: Expect light, bready flavors because high levels and a wide variety of pale malts are used to brew this ale. Pair with breaded foods to complement or with sweet foods to contrast.

- Witbier/Wheat: Expect a thick, creamy flavor of wheat because wheat is the predominate grain used in brewing this unfiltered ale. Pair with foods that benefit from the flavors of lemon, orange, and green herbs like parsely.
- Saison: Expect fruity, tart, and sour flavors with a wild nose because this open-fermented Belgian-style ale gathers the wild yeast around the fermentation tank. Pair with foods that benefit from ripe, pungent, tangy, and complex flavors like ripe cheeses, and smoked seafoods.
- Amber: Expect sweet and smoky and maybe floral flavors from this ale because as more roasted amber malts enter the sweet wort boil, the sweet flavors shine through without being overshadowed by spicy hops. Pair with foods that inspire comfort and warmth and benefit from roasting like cheddar cheese, bacon, and pork.
- Brown: Expect mild, nuttier flavors from this ale because darker malts and low hops are used in brewing. Pair with textural foods like crunchy vegetables or pickles that benefit from a smooth balance and foods that are dairy based.
- Pale Ale: Expect a balance of sweetness, light body, and spice because lighter malts and a high level of hops are used. Pair with foods to temper buttery and creamy flavors or to highlight pungent foods like raw onions.
- India Pale Ale (IPA)/Imperial IPA: Expect high levels of bitter and citric spice because a large amount of diverse hops is used in this ale. Hops act as a natural preservative and maintained fresh beer as it was shipped from England on long sea voyages to India, hence the name India Pale Ale. Pair with foods that are spicy.
- Stout: Expect a dry coffee flavor and medium body because the black malts in this ale have been roasted to a dark, almost black color and few hops are added. Pair with foods that are complex but have been tempered by slow roasting or grilling like beefstew or custards.
- Porter: Expect a syrup flavor because a combination of sweet amber and chocolate malts used in this ale creates a sweet, dark, full liquid.

Porter was the preferred break-time drink of porters in eighteenth-century England. Pair with food that has higher levels of sugar like BBQ sauce, pears, or desserts.

- Barleywine: Expect a dried fruit flavor and high alcohol because more sugars, referred to as higher gravity, are used in the fermentation process. This brings the alcohol content to almost that of a wine, hence the name. Sometimes residual sugars remain in the fermenting casks because yeast cannot ferment long enough to digest all of the sugar in the high-alcohol environment. Pair with foods that are extremely bold, highly sugared, gamey, or boozy.
- Strong: Expect flavors of complex fruit and soft texture with high alcohol from this ale. Pair with boozy, sweet, fruity flavors. Pair with dishes in which one flavor dominates so the complexity of the brew can shine through.
- Lambic: Expect sour fruit flavors and high carbonation from this open-fermented ale, which attracts the floral flavors of wild yeast. Pair with foods that work well with champagne like brunch foods, caviar, brined turkey, vinegar pickles, or foods from the sea and are brined or pickled in vinegar or from the sea.

Two important statistics follow each brew introduced. These features are alcohol by volume (ABV) and international bitterness units (IBU). ABV measures the percentage of alcohol present in the volume of the container. IBU measures the prevalence of the hop bitterness in the brew. For example, an India Pale Ale beer could have a 4.8 percent ABV and 85 IBU, meaning that it is low in alcohol and high in hop flavors. A Porter beer could have a 7.5 percent ABV and a 30 IBU, meaning that it is high in alcohol and low in hop flavors.

Using these very basic descriptions as a reference point, continue through the book to the current season's chapter, visit the Hosting a Beer and Cheese Pairing Party chapter, or use the index to source a pairing by ingredient, beer type, or brewery.

CHAPTER 3

Spring

B lossoms hit the trees, pollen hits the nose, and sunshine hits the skin. Signs of cold and winter melt away slowly and nubs of green poke out of the ground. Tender, young, sour, acidic, crunchy, and bright spring flavors are present this time of year in both food and beer. These flavors bridge the gap between winter's hearty, roasty, meaty, starchy, earthy flavors to summer's grilled, fruity, ripe, pungent, and herbal flavors.

As the weather totters between dismal and foggy, to bright and crisp, the palate toggles too, some days craving light and tangy flavors while other days craving creamy and warm flavors. If a sunny day shows its face, the grill is fired up, willing summer to come sooner. If the rain comes back or a late frost hits the ground, slow-cooked, one-pot dishes hit home.

Spring beer flavors are the high trills and trumpets of a symphony. The spring beer songs tend to be the trumpets with a maltier, or thicker, mouthfeel than a light summer beer. Whereas winter beers rely on booming drums with darker malts and result in thick, coating textures, spring beers use lighter high-pitched malts that lead to a still thick mouthfeel, but a fresh and creamy texture, moving from tip of tongue to throat, fast as a trombone player's elbow, moving the slide in and out. Where dark beers might coat the mouth like molasses, spring beers would coat the mouth like honey, the difference being a much lighter, thinner, and brighter flavor. On the piano, spring beers would be the high notes, trilling in high, quick patterns, using ingredients like lime leaf, white pepper, underripe sour fruit, grass, almond, and rose petal. Special sour yeast strains and hops are introduced to add a slightly sour aromatic appeal, like the light rot of a Parmesan cheese versus winter's sour fragrance of a blue cheese. As beers transition into summer, the summer symphony conductor waves these hops in with more force and tempers the sour yeast strain section to build strong summer brews, ripe like the fruits, herbs, and berries of the season. The conductor then eases the hops down through the fall to showcase the sounds of sweet, toasted, thick, malty brews for the winter.

The original German spring beers were lagers, cold brewed and stored for most of the winter. One example is a "Maibock," "Mai" meaning released in May and "bock" meaning goat as in kick of a goat. (Kick because these beers were fermented a little longer to increase the alcohol, giving a nice kick to spring.) Maibock is served in a footed Pilsner glass. The German Kölsch beer is a traditional cold-brewed spring ale with lower alcohol content than a Maibock. Kölsch is served in a tall, cylindrical glass to preserve the high effervescence of the brew. These spring brews are best sourced at quality beer bars, in variety packs at specialty bottle shops, or at the brewery. They are now becoming more available in standard grocery selection.

SPRING PICKLES

Pickling is very easy to do and also very easy to do incorrectly. The basic rule of pickling safety is threefold: (1) understand that metal and salt can cause a dangerous reaction, which means only glass bowls and canning jars can be used in the process with the exception of a two-piece canning lid with rubber seal, (2) high levels of acid, like a vinegar or citrus must be present to preserve for an extended period of time to prevent botulism, and (3) most styles of pickling require that the cans be sealed properly using heat or pressure to store for an extended time. *The Joy of Pickling* is a user-friendly, detailed guide to safe preserving at home. While food blogs and online recipes show creativity in preserving food, trust tested cookbooks and well-known authors for your safety. Late summer and early fall are when most preserving is done to capture the bounty of produce available at the time. In spring, however, celebrate the tender, sour, and bright new flavors with quick pickling methods that avoid these dangerous pitfalls and better highlight the tender flavors of the season.

	Fresh herbs—mixture of lavender, rosemary, and bay
4	handfuls fresh produce (radish, fennel, asparagus, green onion bulbs, carrots)
1	tablespoon peppercorns
1	tablespoon fennel seeds
1	tablespoon juniper berries
4	tablespoons pickling salt
3	cups white vinegar
1	cup citrus juice
	Large pinch white sugar

(continued)

Prepare the fresh herbs and produce to pickle. Gather a mixture of produce that is available and fresh: radish, fennel bulbs, asparagus stalks, green onion bulbs, citrus, and boldly colored carrots. Pull lavender stems, rosemary, and bay from the garden. Stock up on savory dry herbs with multicolored peppercorns, fennel seeds, and juniper berries. Purchase pickling salt and white wine vinegar to complete the actual pickle process. Pickling salt has no iodine in it and dissolves quickly in warm liquid. Do not substitute another salt or the pickling solution may be cloudy or the salt may not dissolve enough to preserve the food. Have either glass jars or large food-safe freezer-grade plastic bags ready to fill with produce and hot liquid. Two-piece canning lids are fine to seal the jars but are not necessary because this is a two- to three-day quick pickle. A lid is required, however, for each jar. Save old sauce jars for this use to avoid the cost of new canning supplies.

Rinse and pat the fresh herbs dry. Prick the produce all over with a fork and trim it into attractive pieces. Peel the carrots and cut them in half or quarters lengthwise so all carrots pieces are the same size. Remove the stem and bottom tail from the radish and cut each in half. Cut the green onion bulbs in half lengthwise and reserve the dark green stalks for another use. Remove the fronds from the fennel and chop the bulb at an angle to create large circles, a quarter inch in diameter. A fennel bulb is constructed like celery. The part to chop feels like the stalk of celery, thick with strands running through at the base of the plant. Fronds are the wispy green tops that come out of the top, in a similar shape and color as dill. Hold the top and bottom of each asparagus stalk and snap it. It will break a third of the way between the base and the top, eliminating the dry, grainy part. Discard the base and reserve the top. Slice some of the citrus into circles and zest some of the other citrus, avoiding the white pith under the citric peel, and then juice the citrus after zesting.

Place the produce and fresh herbs into a large glass or ceramic bowl or baking dish. Use about a tablespoon of pickling salt per handful of produce. Mix the salt with the produce using your hands or a wooden spoon until coated. The veggies will start to release some juices. Do not use a metal bowl or mixing instrument. Although it is unlikely that a reaction between the salt and the metal will occur, best practices in preserving are to omit metal. Crush dry herbs, juniper, peppercorns, and fennel seeds on a cutting board with a knife. Bring vinegar, 1 cup water, citrus juice, crushed dry herbs, and a pinch of sugar to a slow boil. Stir until sugar is dissolved.

Load the jars or bags up with produce and fresh herbs. If using jars, leave about a half inch between the top of the jar and the top of the produce. If using bags, ensure that there is enough liquid to fill the bag completely so the produce is covered. Pour the warm liquid over the produce. Cover the produce entirely if it is in a bag or jar. If using a jar, cap right away. If using a bag, close almost entirely and let the steam vent out a small crack for about a half hour before sealing. Store the produce while pickling in the fridge for 2 to 3 days. Then strain the produce and give it a light rinse in cold water. Serve with cured meats and cheeses as an appetizer or toss in a vinaigrette of pickling liquid whisked with mustard, honey, and olive oil and serve on a bed of spring lettuce.

Each handful will feed two to four people as part of an appetizer platter and two people on a small salad.

(*continued*)

Beer Pairing

Pair these spring pickles with a Maibock or sharp Pilsner that is light in body and assertive in hop character to stand up to the vinegar flavor. Gordon Biersch Brewing offers a Maibock (7.3% ABV/25 IBU) that is robust with malt flavors of caramel and dark wood that would balance the high vinegar acidity.

Rogue Brewing offers a Dead Guy Ale Maibock (6.5% ABV/40 IBU) that is a glowing copper, with a fresh dry cedar nose with a grassy floral flavor to complement the crisp pickle and balance a pairing that includes mustard and cured meats. New Belgium Brewing offers a Blue Paddle Pilsner (4.8% ABV/33 IBU) that features four slightly sweet malts and a crispy, biting hop flavor that echoes the texture of the pickles. Serve the Pilsners in a tall pint glass and the Maibocks in a tulip glass.

GREEN TOMATO-TOMATILLO JAM

To begin making a jam or sauce with fruit, be it peaches, pears, or tomatoes, the basic formula is as follows. First dice the fruit, give it a hearty sprinkle of sugar, and let it sit for a few hours at room temperature in a nonmetallic dish, per the safety precautions discussed in the Spring Pickles recipe. After a few hours, the sugar releases the natural juices in the fruit and dissolves into the juice. Pour the fruit and its juices into a heavy-bottomed nonstick saucepan, add the spices that will be used, bring to a simmer, and allow to cook on very low for several hours until thick.

- 1 **cup raw cane sugar**
- 3 **pounds green tomatoes or tomatillos (husks and stems removed)**
- 1 **tablespoon cloves**
- 2 **cinnamon sticks**
- 1 **lemon (juice and rind separated)**

To bring out the bright, slightly sour and clove flavors in a German-style Kölsch beer, this jam recipe calls for either green tomatoes, tomatillos, or a combination of both, stewed with cloves, cinnamon, and lemon. Dice green tomatoes or remove tomatillos from their husks and dice. Reserve a quarter of the diced fruit to add later in the process. Place three-fourths of the diced fruit in a glass bowl covered in natural cane sugar. Let sit covered at room temperature for 3 hours. Pour the sugared fruit into a heavy-bottomed pan

(continued)

and add spices, still reserving the ¼ diced unsugared fruit. Add cloves, cinnamon, and lemon rind and juice. Bring to a simmer and turn the heat down as low as possible. Stir with a wooden spoon or plastic spatula often until the jam is thick, about 1 to 2 hours. The jam will stick to the base of the pot a little, but if the jam starts to burn or more and more is sticking to the bottom or side of the pan, add ⅓ cup water as needed. Add the reserved fruit, salt, and remove the cinnamon. Cook another 30 minutes over medium low to integrate the new fruit. Use caution so as to avoid burning the bottom of the jam. If needed, add ¼ cup water.

Remove from the heat and refrigerate until thick. Serve on rye toast with sour cream, crème fraîche, or Mexican crema. Use within a few weeks.

Beer Pairing

Pair with high-hopped, light body, crisp Pilsner. Trumer Pils (4.9% ABV/22 IBU) uses a 400-year-old Austrian recipe to develop flavors of white pepper, nutmeg, and spice. The nose is citric with a light body. Serve this beer in a champagne flute or tall pilsner glass.

ROMANTIC BEER AND CHOCOLATE PAIRING

Deep red wines have long been associated with chocolates, but beer and chocolate age through such similar processes that they are also a natural pairing. Chocolate and malts must dry and age before use. Cacao beans are ground and roasted, similar to the roasted dark grains used in stouts and porters. Both cacao and malts become chocolate and beer through a fermentation process. Note that all beers here are low IBU.

- North Coast Brewing Company's Acme Pale Ale (5% ABV/21 IBU): Pair this crisp, bright pale with a sweet, mild basil-filled milk chocolate to enjoy grassy flavors and smooth textures. This beer also pairs well with mild Thai noodle dishes.
- The Lost Abbey's Carnivale (6.5% ABV): Pair this sweet, effervescent, sour Saison with a salted caramel to enjoy flavors of melon. This beer also pairs well with fruit custards.
- Mammoth Brewing's Nut Brown (5.5% ABV/25 IBU): Pair this black velvet, chocolate-flavored porter with 70% dark chocolate fruit and nut bark to enjoy flavors of burnt hazelnut or chargrilled chestnuts. This beer also pairs well with Nutella.
- North Coast Brewing Company's Brother Thelonious (9.4% ABV/32 IBU): Pair this Belgian-style strong dark ale with rum raisin chocolates to enjoy a flavor of vanilla and pipe tobacco. This beer also pairs well with lavender.
- Drakes Brewing's Drakonic (8.75% ABV/40 IBU): Pair this midnight-black licorice heavy imperial stout with an orange citrus chocolate to enjoy flavors of burnt marshmallow and coffee.

GREEN GARLIC SOUFFLÉ WITH ROASTED ASPARAGUS

As with making pickles, a soufflé is easy to do and also easy to do incorrectly. Victorian corseted women with weak constitutions need not apply. Be passionate and assertive while baking soufflés but do not be emotional. Most likely, every few attempts at soufflé will fail, especially at the beginning. Do not be discouraged; once soufflé success comes regularly, the reward of salty cheese mixed with lighter-than-air eggs, creamy butter, and the bite of green garlic is worth every bit of angst. This recipe will provide an appetizer for four or an entrée for two.

1	bunch asparagus
2–4	tablespoons extra-virgin olive oil
2	tablespoons sea salt
1	lemon or orange
	Pepper (fresh ground to taste)
4	large eggs
½	stick butter
1	tablespoon finely grated Parmesan or flour or Gruyère
3	quarter-size chunks green garlic bulb
1	tablespoon sesame oil (optional)

Green garlic is a late spring treat. Garlic grows in a large bulb, under the soil with a large stalk sticking out, similar to an onion. During growth, garlic transitions from one large bulb to a bulb housing individual cloves. Similar again to an onion, garlic is removed from the ground when full grown to be aged in the air until dried with flaking skin. Green garlic is pulled from the ground before the cloves separate into individual nubs and looks like a green onion. The flavor is more like grass than garlic but hints of the acidic, pungent, familiar garlic flavor are present.

Roasting asparagus is beyond easy. Rinse, dry, and break the asparagus on the bottom third as in the above pickling recipe. Discard the woodsy bottom thirds and toss the remaining stalk with good extra-virgin olive oil and large shards of kosher salt or sea salt. Squeeze a lemon or orange on the asparagus and roast at 400 degrees for 15 to 20 minutes on a baking sheet in a single layer until wilted, bright green with tinges of brown, and tender when prodded with a fork. Remove, cool, and drizzle with a bit of sesame oil to highlight the nuttiness of the asparagus and add a bit of pepper or Parmesan. Turn the oven down to 350 degrees.

While the asparagus is roasting, gather the soufflé ingredients: 4 eggs, a stalk of green garlic (finely dice half, reserve other half in large chunks), 4 individual ramekins or 2 larger individual ramekins, a half stick of butter, flour, grated Parmesan or Gruyère cheese, a very clean metal bowl that has been chilled for 15 minutes in the refrigerator for whites, a whisk or stand mixer, a yolk bowl, and a small bowl to separate the whites into before transferring to the chilled bowl. To make a soufflé, understand that a clear separation of yolk and white is critical. Egg whites are all protein; yolks are a mixture of protein and fat. If even a drizzle of yellow yolk fat is in the egg whites when they are whipped, they will not achieve the nirvana lighter-than-air state. They will most likely not whip fully or fall in the oven while baking. For the best luck in separating an egg, start with a cage-free, vegetarian-fed organic egg. The yolks in these eggs are vibrant

(continued)

yellow and much easier to detect, event in small amounts. Allowing the bird to free range rather than sit still and force feed lowers the levels of fat in their eggs, again improving your chances of whipping only protein.

Resist the urge to crack the egg against the corner of the counter or a bowl. The shell is more likely to shatter into fragments. Crack it against a flat counter or cutting board surface with one strong even crack, then turn the crack up toward you, and place the small bowl under the egg. Tiny repeated cracks will develop small fragments of shell that will fall into the egg when separating. Use both thumbs to open the egg in half like a book, and then tip it to one side, then the other, then the other. Use the small bowl to drip the white into while moving the yolk back and forth between the two egg shell halves. Once the white and yolk are fully separated, and the yolk is in the egg shell and the white in the bowl, move the white to the chilled metal bowl. The importance of a clean bowl for the whites cannot be overstated. If trace amounts of fat are in the bowl, the whites will not whip properly. However, a bit of whites in the yolk is not desirable as those whites avoid being whipped fully, but it is not detrimental. Repeat with the remaining eggs, each time using a small bowl to drip the whites into before moving them to the mixing bowl. This ensures that if shell and yolk infiltrate the whites on egg number three, they do not transfer into the bowl with the two other clean whites. Reserve the yolks in a different clean bowl; they will be used later.

At this point, rub butter and the large chunks of green garlic on the bottom and sides of the ramekins. Not all butter will be used. Discard the garlic. Dust the interior of the dishes with flour or cheese. Place the ramekins on a baking tray very close to the oven to reduce movement between filling the ramekins with egg and putting them into the oven.

Whip the egg whites until stiff peaks form, either by hand with a whisk, in a stand mixer on medium low, or with a hand-held mixer on medium. This will take 3 to 10 minutes. In a separate bowl, whisk the yolks with the finely chopped green garlic until mixed. This will take less than a minute. Fold the fluffy whites into the yolks using a spatula. The more the yolk and white are mixed, the more they risk falling. Just fold until combined. Place the mixture into the ramekins. Then place the ramekins into the oven. Bake until puffed, lightly golden; a skewer inserted into the middle of a soufflé comes out with dry bits stuck to it or clean. Depending on the size of ramekins, the soufflé will take 6 to 15 minutes. If it takes longer, check every 1-2 minutes to avoid overcooking.

Serve soufflé with the side of roasted asparagus. The soufflé will deflate if covered or with time, so eat it quickly after removing from the oven.

Beer Pairing

Pair with golden brews that are light in IBU. Mammoth Brewing's Golden Trout Pilsner (5.5% ABV/30 IBU) combines a light malty body created with Pilsner and Vienna malts with a floral Sterling hop finish that mimics the light pungency of the green garlic. North Coast Brewing Company's Scrimshaw Pilsner (4.9% ABV/22 IBU) offers a malty effervescence and traditional Saaz hops that will accentuate the nutty asparagus. Serve these brews in chilled pilsner glasses to best highlight the pairing.

GEWÜRZTRAMINER
SPLIT PEA SOUP WITH HAM

Slow-cooking legume soups like split pea are for long spring weekends, when the wind is blustery, the sun is absent, and the air is moist. Spend the day inside, tending to this low-maintenance soup and be rewarded with a warm, thick, fragrant meal. This is an excellent way to heal a spring cold or to use the remaining ham from spring holidays.

Selecting the ham used for the soup will make or break the flavor. Using the large center bone is very important to develop a thick broth. As the broth simmers for hours, bone marrow, gelatins, calcium, and other minerals leave the bone and infuse the water.

This recipe will fill at least four hearty bowls.

1 package split peas
2 cups stock ingredients (discarded parts of carrots, parsley, onion, celery, garlic, peppercorns, bay leaves)
1 large ham bone
1 bunch fresh thyme
½ bottle Gewürztraminer
1 cup chopped ham
   Squeeze from 1 lemon wedge
1 teaspoon salt

Either green or yellow split peas can be used. Split peas are not actually a dried pea split in half; they are a legume, similar in shape to a lentil. Rinse and drain the split peas, removing any discolored or chipped peas. In our freezer, we reserve bones and the discarded peelings and pieces of organic carrots, onions, celery, garlic, and herbs. When chopping a salad or making a sauce, save the carrot shavings, parsley stems, onion skins, and other parts and pieces and toss them into a freezer bag and store until ready to make soup. Store the rind of hard cheeses there as well to use as a thickening agent in beans and soups. Gather a ham bone and these aromatics either from your freezer or use 4 large carrots, a bunch of parsley, 4 stalks of celery, 2 white onions cut in half, 10 peppercorns, and 3 garlic cloves. The carcass of a chicken can be added in place of the ham bone to make chicken stock as well. To make a spicy pork broth, include 1 or 2 dried chiles.

Place into a large stock pot with the bone on the bottom and cover with 8 cups cold, filtered water. Bring to a simmer. Skim the top every 15 minutes for 1 hour, removing the scum that bubbles to the top. Continue to cook for at least 6 hours, adding more water as needed to keep veggies and bone covered.

At hour 6, strain the broth, reserving only the liquid. Add the rinsed split peas, salt, and bring to a simmer until the peas dissolve, around 50 minutes. At minute 40, add Gewürztraminer and thyme. Gewurztraminer is a German-style white wine. It is sweet but crisp and tastes like a green apple blossom. In selecting the wine, pick something that is crisp and thin, not syrupy and overly sweet, so it adds aroma more than flavor and does not overshadow the beer. Bring to a boil until minute 50, stirring often to prevent peas from burning on bottom. Add chopped ham, fresh thyme, and a squeeze of lemon and remove from the heat.

(continued)

Beer Pairing

Pair this soup with an American version of an English Brown Ale in a beer mug. Lost Coast Brewing's Downtown Brown (5% ABV/14 IBU) offers a silky smooth body that mimics the creaminess of the soup. The beer can be drunk at 50 to 55 degrees, preventing the tooth-shattering pain of moving from a cold drink to a hot soup. The floral nose of the brew will increase the flavor of the Gewürztraminer and thyme. The light-brown body offers a deep ruby color, lasting white ring of head, and earthy hop finish that agrees with the ham.

CRABS

Crabs should be caught or bought alive on the day that they will be cooked. Crabs that are not moving or have damaged shells are not fresh. Do not store crabs in water: they will drown from lack of oxygen. Store them in a cool and dry place like the fridge or an ice chest on top of a bed of ice but not submerged in the ice. If the idea of their claws fighting back while they are cooking is unnerving, place them in the freezer for 15 minutes before steaming or boiling to reduce movement. These methods of cooking and cleaning crab work for blue crabs found in the East Coast, Dungeness crabs from the West Coast, and Jonah "Maine" crabs. Soft shell crabs are cleaned differently and require sautéing rather than water cooking. King and Snow crabs are in such high demand that they are usually sold cooked and cleaned as leg meat only. In that case, skip to the sauce section of the recipe. Consider using the Monterey Bay Aquarium seafood watch guide found on their website when selecting a crab type. King and Snow crab populations are almost at dangerously low populations. Selecting the other types of crabs listed on this guide is more sustainable.

> **Crabs, 1–2 per person**
> **Either boil in Old Bay seasoning (⅓ cup) or**
> **in lemon (2 lemons cut into rings)**
> **Additional ingredients based on the sauce and**
> **beer selection chosen (see below)**

Fill the pot with enough water to cover all the crabs by more than two fingers and bring it to such a rolling boil that it looks like waves of the ocean.

(continued)

Then add the Old Bay seasoning, and less than a minute later, add the crabs so that as the seasoning dissolves into the water, it coats the crabs. Boil until bright pink and remove, then cool the crabs in a single layer. If stacked while cooling, the crabs will continue to steam and cook.

If steaming, combine lemons cut into rings with a healthy handful of salt and water. The water should be salted enough to taste of the sea to preserve the integrity of the crab's flavor. Taste the water; it should be as salty as seawater with a fragrant bite of lemon. Bring it to boil and place a steam tray above the water. Place the crabs in the tray, cover them, and steam in a single layer until pink. Cool in a single layer. If stacked as it cools, the crabs will continue to steam and cook.

To clean crabs, prepare a discard bowl, a small bowl of water to rinse bits of shell off your fingers, a small bowl for the mustard, and a large bowl for crab meat or pieces to eat. Remove the legs and claws. Either crack these pieces open and add the shell to the discard bowl and meat to the eating bowl, or break the legs at the joints and add these smaller pieces of leg and claw to the eating bowl for guests to crack while eating. Rinse and dry hands in between to make the project less slippery. With the legs removed, place the crab belly side up in one open palm, and with the other hand, pull off the apron. The apron is triangle-shaped and goes from the edge to the middle of the stomach. Grab the point of the triangle in the midstomach and pull it back toward the edge until it breaks off. Place in the disposal bowl. Grasping the crab in an open palm, separate the bottom shell from the top shell, lifting one clean off the other. Discard the gills, which look like rows and rows of rubber almonds, and place the green "mustard" or tomalley in your small bowl. This mustard is incredibly flavorful when added to sauces and the shell and gills can be reserved to make crab stock or broth.

THAI BUTTER SAUCE

- 1 stick butter, cubed
- ¼ cup water
- 1 lime
- 1–2 dried chiles (depending on spice preference)
- 3 basil leaves

Cut a room-temperature stick of butter into at least 16 cubes. Bring ¼ cup water to a boil with a squeeze of lime, dried chiles, and a few leaves of basil. Strain the chiles and basil; return the now-flavored water to boil. Whisk in the butter, cube by cube, not adding the next cube until the previous one is melted. When combined, remove from heat and dip crab meat. (Similar brews include Fat Tire Amber Ale (5.2% ABV/18.5 IBU) by New Belgium Brewing and Lucky 13 by Lagunitas Brewing Company (8.8% ABV/60 IBU)).

Beer Pairing

Select Rising Moon by Blue Moon Brewing Company (4.3% ABV/15 IBU). This German-style Kölsch with kefir lime leaves pairs with a Thai Butter Sauce. Serve in a champagne flute.

(continued)

COCKTAIL SAUCE

4	tablespoons ketchup
3	tablespoons chili sauce
1	lemon (squeezed)
1	teaspoon Worcestershire sauce
½	teaspoon prepared horseradish
½	teaspoon white pepper
1½	teaspoons celery seed

Combine equal parts ketchup and chili sauce with a squeeze of lemon and Worcestershire, pinch of horseradish, white pepper, and celery seed. Mix and chill before dipping.

Beer Pairing

Select Acme Pale Ale by North Coast Brewing Company (5% ABV/21 IBU) or another mild California Pale Ale to pair with an old-fashioned cocktail sauce. High levels of tomato acid highlight the light spring hops. Serve in a pint glass.

MUSTARD SAUCE

>   Crab "mustard" (as much as is available)
> 2 tablespoons saison
> 2 sprigs fresh thyme
> 2 tablespoons Dijon mustard

Mix the "mustard" that was reserved in the bowl above in a small saucepan with a splash of the saison, a few sprigs of fresh thyme, and the Dijon mustard. Bring to a simmer, whisking until combined and warm. If the amount created is too little for the crab to be eaten, add cubes of butter as indicated in the Thai Sauce recipe above.

Beer Pairing

Select Sierra Nevada Brewing Company's Ovila (7.2% ABV/24 IBU) and create a simple Mustard Sauce to highlight the sweet crab and complex floral saison. Serve in a tulip glass.

CORNED BEEF, GREEN ONION CHAMP, AND CABBAGE

C orned beef is better when you corn it yourself. Commercial corned beef can be doctored by removing it from the package, letting it air dry for 15 minutes, and coating it with a dry rub of salt, juniper berries, mustard, and pickling spices that have been blended in a food processor. Cover and refrigerate overnight. Rinse and then boil per the package's directions. To corn it yourself, plan to start on day one and eat on day five.

1 to 4	pounds brisket (¼–⅓ pound per person)
1½	cups kosher salt
¾	cup organic cane sugar
1	cabbage head
1	bunch carrots, cut in quarter-size pieces

PICKLING INGREDIENTS:

5	garlic cloves
3	tablespoons juniper berries
3	tablespoons pink peppercorns
3	tablespoons whole cloves
3	tablespoons all-spice
3	tablespoons rosemary
3	tablespoons coriander
4	bay leaves

BOILING MIXTURE INGREDIENTS:

2–3	bottles beer
3	star anise

3 garlic cloves
2 tablespoons peppercorns
1 bunch parsley
3 bay leaves
1 white onion (quartered)

BAKING PASTE INGREDIENTS:
⅓ cup honey
⅓ cup mustard

GRAVY INGREDIENTS:
⅓ cup flour
2 tablespoons butter

GREEN ONION CHAMP
5–6 Russet or Yukon Gold potatoes
1 cup whole milk
1 bunch green onions or scallions

To corn beef, buy a brisket and create a brine. Brisket is a tough meat from the chest of the cow. Corning it and cooking it for a long period of time softens the meat. Mix 1 gallon of water with 1½ cups kosher salt, ¾ cup organic cane sugar, 5 whole garlic cloves, and 3 tablespoons each juniper berries, pink peppercorns, whole cloves, allspice berries, rosemary, coriander, and 4 bay leaves. This recipe does not contain nitrates in the form of pink salt. As such, the beef will not be bright pink when cooked. The benefits of

(continued)

nitrates in food do not outweigh the health implications, but if you prefer to include them, *Charcuterie: The Craft of Salting, Smoking, and Curing* offers instruction on safely using this ingredient. Omitting nitrates will shorten the time the cooked meat will last. Store it no more than 2 days. Bring the brine to a simmer in a large pot until dissolved, allow to cool fully, and submerge the brisket for 3 days in the refrigerator. Remove it from the brine and let air dry overnight in the refrigerator before cooking.

Bring the beer you are using to a boil and add the corned beef to the pot. It will take 2 to 3 bottles. One-fourth cup spicy pickle juice can be added to the pot as well to add a zesty tang to the meat. The kitchen will be very pungent while cooking if pickle juice is added. Add 3 each: star anise, garlic cloves, plus 2 tablespoons peppercorns, a bunch of fresh parsley, 3 bay leaves, and a quartered white onion. Return to a boil and simmer for 3 hours. Cool and refrigerate for 24 hours in the liquid. Return to a boil, remove the meat from the pan, and put it into a baking dish. Form a paste with ⅓ cup each honey and mustard. Coat and bake it at 325 degrees for 30 minutes. In the boiling liquid, add a head of cabbage that has been quartered and a bunch of carrots cut into coins. Simmer for 30 minutes while the beef is baking.

Remove the beef and place on a platter. Remove the veggies from the broth with a slotted spoon and add to the platter. Add ⅓ cup flour and 2 tablespoons butter to the broth. Stir until thickened and turn off the heat. Pour the gravy over the platter.

Champ is an Irish dish made of green onion-scented mashed potatoes. The French have a similar dish, called *pommes dauphinoise*, where potatoes are sliced and baked in garlic-scented milk.

To make authentic Champ, select potatoes high in starch like Russet or Yukon Gold. Use 5 to 6 potatoes. Although smaller and red potatoes are excellent for high-heat roasting because the high heat develops their sugars, they make less desirable mashed potatoes because they are not smooth when mashed. Scrub the potato skins in cold water. Drop them into boiling water and boil until soft. To test their doneness, poke them with a fork. The fork should go in and out effortlessly. Meanwhile, chop some green onions or scallions and place them into a pot with cold whole milk. Use about a bunch of scallions to 1 cup milk per 5 potatoes. Bring the onion milk to simmer for a few minutes, then turn off the heat and let the onions infuse the milk, still covered.

Let the potatoes cool, and then remove their skins. The warmer they are, the easier the skins will be to remove. Use a ricer, food processor, or blender to mash the potatoes. Mix the warm milk and onions with the mashed potatoes. Add about 3 tablespoons butter per 5 potatoes and a few pinches of white pepper. Place in a baking dish and heat with a little salt at 350 degrees until a light-brown crust forms.

Beer Pairing

Pair corned beef with beers that mimic those of Ireland in pint glasses. Anchor Brewing's Anchor Bock (5.5% ABV/24 IBU) is brown with notes of licorice and nut spice and hints of citrus to highlight the mustards that corned beef are often served with.

GRASS-FED FILLET WITH ROASTED FINGERLING POTATOES

The discussion about free-range grass-fed beef versus grass-finished beef versus corn-fed beef has been made much more complex than it need be. Cows were meant to have room to graze and eat a diet of what they find in the pasture. Just as the human body is in better shape when allowed to exercise, eat well, and live in nonstressful conditions, the best flavor in protein comes when the animal is allowed room to move about and graze slowly on natural feed because it slowly builds muscle and fat, offering cuts marbled with delicious muscle and fat rather than tough muscle or excess fat. Corn-fed beef is not a bad thing: most beef receives some grain—it bulks the animal up quickly and efficiently for maximum production, but maximum flavor in the animal develops with a diet of grass, which its body is better equipped to digest and process. Room to roam and a nonstressful environment are important for two reasons: they allow the animal to build muscle slowly, thus making it tender and marbled, and fewer stress hormones are present in the animal, meaning the muscles are less rigid and tough.

1	fillet or ½ pound fillet tip per person
5	fingerling potatoes per person
2	tablespoons prepared herbes de provence per person (or equal parts basil, thyme, savory, lavender)
2	garlic cloves per person
1–2	tablespoons Worcestershire sauce per fillet or per person
2	tablespoons butter per person
	Olive oil (4 tablespoons for potatoes, 2 tablespoons per fillet or per person)

¼ cup beef or chicken broth
2 tablespoons cream per person
1 tablespoon butter per person

In preparing your fillet and roasted potatoes, purchase a fillet or fillet tip cut from your farmer or a trusted butcher. Look for meat that has not been frozen and has beautiful marbling. It should be pink, almost purple with thread-fine lines of white running through it. This cut will be expensive, and because the fillet has no connective tissues, it makes it incredibly tender. If you buy a fillet tip, it will be shaped like a thick carrot, slowly whittling down from thick to thin. Leave it intact. If you purchase individually cut fillets, they will be round or egg shaped and ½ to 2 inches thick. Plan for a fillet per person or ½ to 1 pound per person. Ask your butcher to cut fillets by number needed, not by weight. Allow the butcher's expertise to guide the cut size.

Place the meat in a glass dish that can be covered with plastic wrap or a food-safe bag that can seal securely. Coat the meat in a sprinkle of salt, then rub it aggressively with the 2 tablespoons herbes de provence. To make herbes de provence, mix fresh chopped basil, thyme, savory, and lavender. The dry spice blend can be purchased already mixed as well. Place the meat in the dish or bag and add 2 rough chopped cloves of garlic per person. Pour 1 to 2 tablespoons of Worcestershire sauce, which features the savory, salty flavor of molasses, juniper berries, anchovies, and spices. Allow the meat to marinate in the flavors for at least 24 hours in the refrigerator.

(continued)

When the steaks have been marinated, start cooking an hour before eating. To roast the meat, preheat the oven to 400 degrees. Roasting will seal the outside of the food, especially if coated in a fatlike olive oil, and the interior of the food will become sweet and tender. The high temperature develops the sugars in the food and can burn if unattended. Take the steak from the fridge and allow it to come to room temperature.

Fingerling potatoes are shaped like fingers (per their namesake) and are small, sweet, and pale yellow. Small red potatoes may be substituted but will lack the sweetness of the fingerlings. Coat the fingerling potatoes, 5 or so per person, in olive oil, salt, and 1 teaspoon herbes de provence. Duck fat can replace the olive oil for extra crispy potatoes. Place them on a baking sheet in a single layer, not touching, in the oven. If they touch, they will not achieve a crispy outside and tender sweet inside; they will instead steam and possibly become soggy. The fingerlings are done when they are fork tender, which may take 30 to 45 minutes, more if your oven temperature varies or you are cooking at a high elevation.

In an oven-safe skillet, heat an equal mixture of butter and olive oil until melted over medium-high heat to sear the fillet. Two tablespoons of each is a good ratio. Olive oil has a higher smoke point than butter, and combining the two allows the nutty flavor of the butter and rich coating of the oil to infuse into the steak without burning. Once the butter is bubbling, place the fillet tip or fillet into the pan and leave it alone. There is no benefit to moving the meat; it will just tear. The goal is to achieve a brown crust on each side of the fillets. Once each side is browned, flip to the next side. Remove fillets and rest on a plate if room is needed in the skillet to brown all pieces. Once all sides of all cuts have browned, return meat to the pan adding an extra skillet if needed so the cuts of meat do not touch. Place the skillets in the oven for 5 to 15 minutes, until the internal temperature of the meat hits the desired doneness (125 degrees for rare, 135 degrees for medium, 145 degrees for well). If using a fillet tip, check the thinner and thicker sides of the meat as their temperatures will vary slightly. Meat will continue to cook after leaving the oven and will rise by 3–6 degrees.

Remove the skillets and allow the meat to rest on a room-temperature surface for at least 5 minutes before cutting. Do not cover the meat or it will steam off the crust. Add beef or chicken broth to the pan over medium heat, scraping the pan with a wooden spoon to remove the burnt bits. Add a sprinkle of herbes de provence and allow the sauce to reduce by half. Remove from the heat, add a pat of butter and a dash of cream, whisk, and pour over your cut fillet. Serve roasted potatoes along side with a drizzle of pan sauce.

Beer Pairing

Pair the steak with a low-hopped, robust pale ale in a pint glass. Ballast Point Brewing Company's Pale Ale (4.6% ABV/23 IBU) is brewed at a warmer temperature, creating a fruity, slightly spicy brew that works well with the herbes de provence.

MEYER LEMON CURD

Lemons embody spring with their bright color, sour flavor, and pungent fragrance. Meyer lemons are less sour, juicer, and zestier than other varieties of lemons. This is a great citrus to grow in dwarf form if space is limited because it requires little water and lots of sun to produce large fruit.

4	Meyer lemons
½	cup organic cane sugar
2	large, cage-free eggs
1	stick unsalted sweet cream butter

Bring the butter to room temperature and cut it into 6 equal-sized pieces. Zest at least 2 tablespoons from the lemons and finely chop the zest. Juice at least ½ cup juice from the lemons. Always zest before juicing; it is much easier to remove the zest while the fruit is intact.

Bring a saucepan of water to a very gentle boil. Place a metal bowl on top to create a double boiler. A double boiler allows the substance in the top bowl to be heated by the steam from the saucepan without receiving direct heat. In the metal bowl, place the zest, juice, sugar, and eggs. Whisk until combined; use a hot pad to avoid a steam burn as the bowl will become very warm. Add the butter, 1 chunk at a time, whisking until smooth. Bring the temperature to 160 degrees. Remove from the heat and cover with waxed paper. Serve the curd warm or cool on cake, pastries, or cookies.

If the eggs scramble, the water is too hot. If lemons are unavailable, use grapefruit or oranges.

Beer Pairing

Pair this tangy sweet curd with high complex strong or wheat beers. Russian River Brewing's Damnation Strong Ale (7.75% ABV/25 IBU) is golden in color and banana on the nose with a dry, spicy finish. This brew would be a strong pairing with a lemon curd–topped shortbread cookie. Dunk the cookie in the beer in a brandy glass. Allagash Brewing Company's Witbier White (5.2% ABV/28 IBU) has flavors of citrus, coriander, cloves, and tangy orange peel. This brew will highlight the pungent lemon but offer a tempering herbal flavor. Use a tulip glass.

ELDERFLOWER BROWN BEER COCKTAIL

S t. Germain is liquor made from the elderflower. The elderflower blooms for just a few short weeks in late spring, and when harvested, extracted, and added to the liquor, the blossoms impart a floral fragrance similar to rosewater and a light peach and honey flavor to the liquor. St. Germain is a wonderful addition to brown ale, gin, soda water, and champagne.

For this cross-continental spring cocktail, we mix an American Brown Ale with European St. Germain and Australian finger lime. In selecting a brown for this cocktail, look for an American-produced Brown Ale with a light body and roasted aged teakwood color. Lost Coast Brewing Company in Eureka, California, produces Downtown Brown Ale (5% ABV/14 IBU), which is actually a riff on an English-style Brown with light American mouthfeel and a slight nuttiness that works well. Rogue Ales in Newport, Oregon, produces a very interesting Hazelnut Brown Nectar (6%+ ABV/33 IBU) that is less sweet than Lost Coast's and offers a very nutty fragrance to add to the floral nose of the elderflower. Avoid a true English brown with darker or rust-colored ale like a Newcastle. Although this is a great beer, the thick, syrupy mouthfeel is too dominant to let the delicate liquor shine.

Australian finger lime is a newly available citrus. Distribution of the actual fruit seems limited, but growers in Winters, California, and other areas sell the plant itself. In most regions, the fruit produces only in the fall. If access is limited in your area, substitute any lime. What differentiates this lime is a long skinny finger shape, and rather than shards or strings of pulp inside the rind like most citrus, the finger lime has small caviar-size balls of pulp that burst when compressed. We prefer the finger lime for this spring cocktail because as the small balls of citrus are drunk, they pop in sharp, citric bursts, echoing the acidic and bright flavors of spring.

To mix the cocktail, gently remove the pulp from the finger lime and place into the bottom of a tulip glass. Pour a shot of elderflower liquor on top and let rest for a moment to integrate. Pour the beer down the side of the brew to gently stir the lime pulp to the top of the glass. Enjoy flavors of a boozy cream soda.

CHAPTER 4

Summer

W aves of heat bring ripe fruit, cravings for refreshing foods, and grilled meats. Bold, fruity, creamy, chilled, herbal, and raw flavors are present this time of year in both food and beer. These flavors develop the acidic and crunchy flavors of spring into ripe and pungent. Before the salty, yeasty, and nutty flavors of fall enter the palate, the flavors of summer offer a mix of hydrating, light, and fruity flavors.

Summer beers are the sounds of a marching band, with high-energy percussion drums, tubas, and clanging percussion instruments all moving in high-volume repetition. Summer beer songs feature a light, refreshing mouthfeel and appearance. High hops clang and dominate the soundtrack with citric, rosemary, and herbal notes on the nose. Repetitive tubas keep marchers moving with cloudy blonde and roasted amber textures. Leading the marching band, twirling batons wave sour flavors aside and welcome in fruity, hoppy, and ripe flavors.

Hefeweizen and India Pale Ale (IPA) are summer brews. Hefeweizen is made using malted wheat in place of barley or rye. This brew is unfiltered, cloudy, and creamy and has tart, grainy flavors. IPA is a heavily hopped brew. Hops are a natural preservative that were added by British brewers to make the trip to India and still be fresh upon arrival for the settlers. The end result is big, bright, bold flavors of citrus, grapefruit, and evergreen tree such as juniper and pine. This contributes a pronounced "bitter" flavor.

HONEY GRILLED APRICOTS, AGED WHITE CHEDDAR, AND CHIMICHURRI

This recipe and beer pairing create a perfect balance of textures between smooth beers, hard stone fruit with soft grilled sides, and crumbly aged white cheddar and oily sauce and a perfect balance of flavors with fruity-sour fruit and beers, sweet honey, dry cheese, and pungent herbal sauce.

4   peaches or apricots
7   tablespoons whipped honey
½   cup extra-virgin olive oil
2   tablespoons vinegar
1   cup flat leaf parsley (leaves only)
½   cup cilantro (leaves only)
1   garlic clove
    Salt and pepper
⅓   pound aged white cheddar
    Pinch red pepper flakes

Heat a grill surface until it smokes when rubbed with olive oil. Meanwile, slice the fruit into thick wedges. Use a sharp, unserrated knife. (Serrated knives should be used only on things with squishy interiors like tomatoes, very ripe fruit, and bread. The rivets in the knives break the surface without squishing the inside.) Hold the fruit on one side, place the blade of the knife into the fruit, and rotate the fruit around slowly to form a cut ring around the outside. Repeat the process multiple times to cut wedges. Coat the fruit with a creamy honey on both cut surfaces. If the fruit is overripe, this will be difficult because the meat will squish under the honey. Place the fruit in the fridge for at least 15 minutes so that the honey hardens on the fruit and stays on the fruit on the grill.

Make the chimichurri sauce. Mix olive oil, vinegar, herbs, and garlic until a uniform sauce. The sauce will have a chunky texture and a tangy, pungent taste. Add salt, pepper, and a pinch of red pepper flakes to brighten the sauce further. To use a mortar and pestle, start by mashing the garlic and herbs together into a paste. To use a blender or food processor, just toss it all in. Mix to taste.

Thinly shave the aged white cheddar to prepare to melt it on the fruit. The fruit does not need to be "cooked" on the grill; this process is more about softening it. Thin slices of cheese help it to melt quickly when it sits on top of the fruit.

Pull the cut fruit from the fridge and place the cut honey-coated sides on the grill. Leave them still for at least 3 minutes until the grill leaves black marks in the fruit. In general, the cooking technique "barbequing" does not require the food being grilled to be shuffled about; that just tears the food. Set it where you want it and leave it alone until it's time to flip it. Do not press down on it with a spatula; this just pushes all the juices out of the food to burn on the grill. Flip the stone fruit to the other cut side, place the thinly sliced white cheddar on the side with grill marks, and leave that still for as long as needed to melt the cheese on top and leave grill marks on the bottom. Remove the slices and drizzle with chimichurri.

Serve warm as an appetizer for 4 to 8 people.

(continued)

Beer Pairing

Pair this recipe with a sour, fruit-forward brew. An ideal complementary pairing would be Pyramid Brewery's Apricot Ale or Dogfish Head Brewing's Festina Peche Ale (5.1% ABU/11% IBU). Apricot Ale leans to the sweet grainy side and is brewed with real apricots with a dry finish that highlights the charred honey. Dogfish Head leans to the sour fruity side and is brewed with open fermentation leading to a more sour flavor. Because both of these beers pair through scent as much as taste, use a tulip-shaped glass that will let the mild but floral taste escape through a large opening.

PEEL AND EAT SHRIMP

The sweet flavor of shrimp is highlighted by the flavors in their shell and head. If preferred, the shrimp can be deveined with heads removed, but the shell and tail should remain on. Highlight the spicy Cajun spices, citric marinate, and oils with a high-hopped summer Pale Ale or focus on the sweet, fresh shrimp with a crispy, acidic pilsner. Select a shrimp large enough so that there are no more than 15 shrimp per pound.

- 1 pound shrimp, deveined with shell on
- 1 bunch parsley, stems only
- ¼ cup celery leaves
- ¼ cup citrus rinds
- 2 garlic cloves, unpeeled
- 1 small onion, unpeeled, quartered
- 2 bay leaves
- 1 tablespoon black peppercorns
- 3 tablespoons butter, cubed
- 2 tablespoons Cajun seasoning

This dish is similar to making stock in that it uses up the less preferred parts of veggies. Herb stems, outer veggie peels, and discarded bases and leaves work well. In a baking dish, combine parsley stems, chopped celery leaves, citrus rind, garlic, onion, bay leaves, black peppercorns, butter, and Cajun seasoning. A pound of shrimp will feed two for dinner or four for appetizers.

(continued)

Store the shrimp in the baking dish in the marinade, covered and chilled for 24 to 48 hours. Preheat the oven to 325 degrees. Move the shrimp directly from the refrigerator to the oven and cook, covered, for about 15 minutes. The shrimp are cooked when they are pink throughout. Remove cover, place shrimp on platter, and pour the now-flavorful butter from the dish through a strainer onto the shrimp.

Beer Pairing

To pair this dish with a Pilsner, select a crisp, bright brew. Trumer Pils (4.9% ABV/26 IBU) has a crisp Bavarian-style hopped backbone, light nutmeg bite, and sweet finish. Although this beer accents the sweet element of the shrimp, it is bold enough to withstand the smoky heat of the spice. This style of beer refreshes the palate from the butter and animal fats in the dish.

A mellow American hopped Pilsner such as North Coast Brewing Company's Scrimshaw Pilsner (4.9% ABV/22 IBU) would work with this dish as well. The malty background of this brew highlights the citrus and pepper flavors infused into the shrimp. Rather than cleanse the palate between bites, this brew will leave a lingering, buttery flavor on the palate.

For a Pilsner that features a malty and hoppy balance, Gordon Biersch Brewing's Pilsner (5.2% ABV/32 IBU) is the best of both worlds. This beer has the maltiness of an American style (Scrimshaw) with the crisp Saaz hop style found in the Trumer.

MANGO CAPRESE WITH HOMEMADE MOZZARELLA

An updated version of the traditional tomato, basil, and mozzarella salad, this mango caprese is designed to pair with summer's high-hopped American Pale Ales.

1   small red onion
1   mango
1   bunch cilantro, leaves only
1   gallon whole milk, organic (not ultra-pasteurized)
6   drops rennet
1   lemon (juice of) or 3 tablespoons white vinegar
3   tablespoons extra-virgin olive oil
    Pinch salt

Thinly slice a red onion. Cut the top and bottom of the onion off, removing the hairy stems. Place one of the now-flat sides down on the cutting surface and cut down the middle from stem to stem, splitting the onion in half. Place the large cut side down on the cutting board and cut thin slices. Toss the onion with salt and 2 to 3 tablespoons of cold-pressed extra-virgin olive oil.

Select a ripe mango. Look for a mostly yellow skin with more green than brown. When pressed, the flesh should have more give than a knuckle but not as much as an inner thigh. Cut the mango into cubes. Cut the mango from tip to tip, in a full circle around the mango. Pull one half away from the other, cutting along the pit to remove the half.

(continued)

Place the skin side down and use a small knife to cut the flesh into a grid producing squares. Push the skin in toward the flesh so that squares pop outward. Cut the squares along the skin and add to the onion. Finely chop the leaves from a bunch of cilantro and add to the mango, onion, olive oil, and salt.

To make fresh mozzarella, heat whole milk in a nonstick heavy pot to 90 degrees. Disolve rennet in ¼ cup cold water and mix into the milk. Maintaining a 90-degree heat, let the mixture sit for 1 hour. Then add the juice of a lemon or the white vinegar, increase heat, and stir until curds begin to form. Remove the curds with a slotted spoon.

Allow the curds to cool then crumble the curds in a glass bowl with 2 tablespoons of salt per pound of mozzarella. Pour enough hot water over the curds to fully submerse the curds. Water should be 175–200 degrees. Using thick gloves, massage the curds in the water for less than 30 seconds until they melt and join into a ball. Lift the curds from the warm water and drop into cold water. The mozzarella can easily be overworked, so the dunk portion should take less than a minute. If it is taking longer, use hotter water.

To serve this dish as an appetizer, pull the mozzarella into bite-sized pieces and combine with mayonnaise, chopped cilantro, and serve as is. To serve this dish as a salad, add a bitter green like arugula and toss with a bit of balsamic vinegar and honey.

Beer Pairing

Pair this dish with a high-hopped American Pale Ale. The rosemary nose and heavy burn will contrast well with the buttery mozzarella, pungent onion, sweet and slippery mango, and herbal cilantro. Alaskan Brewing's Pale Ale (5.2% ABV/24 IBU) has citrus, herbs, and spice on the nose and palate.

To temper the hops and nasal burn of the red onion, try pairing this dish with Redhook Brewing's ESB (extra special bitter) (5.8% ABV/28 IBU). In beer, "bitter" is a flavor descriptor meaning not sweet, not smoky, not burnt, but refreshing and balanced in boldness. This style of brew has the high citric hop character with balanced caramel tones. This brew will add a complex roasted caramel flavor to the dish. Offer in pint or tulip glass.

WHOLE SALT-ROASTED FISH

S alt roasting a whole fish does not impart a salty flavor into the dish; instead it maintains a high level of moisture and creates a beautiful presentation. The devil is in the details on this dish; select a fish that fits the oven and pan it will be cooked in. See chapter 1 notes on "Selecting Ingredients" to select a fresh fish.

1	whole white-fleshed fish
3–4	cups sea salt
5	bay leaves
3	tablespoons peppercorns
¼	cup pitted olives (see pairing note)
1	lemon (zested)
1	egg, white only
	Drizzle cold-pressed extra-virgin olive oil

Clean the inside of the fish, rinse, and pat dry. Most fishmongers and butchers will clean before selling. Leave head, tail, and scales intact. Preheat the oven to 400 degrees. Fill the bottom of a glass baking tray with sea salt and add 3 bay leaves. Lay the fish on top. Stuff the inside of the fish with peppercorns, bay leaves, and olives. Top the fish with 2 more bay leaves.

Zest a lemon and whisk the egg white. Combine zest and egg with about 2 cups sea salt. Pack the mixture on top of the fish to form a hard shell. The tail can remain uncovered. Bake in the middle of the oven for 25 minutes. Crack off the salt and serve with fresh herbs and a drizzle of olive oil.

Beer Pairing

Pair this dish with a wheat summer beer. Boston Beer's Summer Ale (5.3% ABV/7 IBU) will sweeten the citric aroma in the dish with a brewing spice dubbed "Grains of Paradise." Expect a tropical palate with peach, mango and guava. This American wheat ale has the brightness of a Kölsch that mimics the slight sea salt flavor but has a texture that is flakey but dense like the fish.

To add an herbal note to the fish, pair with a Belgian-style Golden Ale. Trade Winds Brewing's Tripel Belgian-style Golden Ale (8% ABV/25 IBU) is brewed with rice for a light texture similar to the light white fish. This brew is spiced with Thai basil, which shows more on the nose than the palate, allowing the juicy, briny fish to shine. The brew's light, sweet body makes the fish meat decadent and juicy. Offer both brews in a casual beer mug, chilled if the weather is warm.

PORK CARNITAS

arnitas is slow-roasted pork shoulder with Hispanic-influenced flavors. This cut is referred to as pork shoulder or pork butt. It is often
served with corn or flour tortillas as a taco or burrito filling over rice and
beans. The slow-roasted milk crust, aromatic cinnamon, and slight hint of
citrus found in the carnitas pairs with creamy summer amber ales.

5	pounds boneless pork shoulder
½	cup coarse sea salt
1	cup broth (chicken, vegetable, or pork)
1	orange, juice
1–3	cups whole milk
1	teaspoon dried oregano
3	dried chiles
2	cinnamon sticks
2	bay leaves
1	teaspoon ground cumin
4	peeled garlic cloves
2	dried hibiscus
	Handful of peppercorns
5–10	banana leaves
1	cucumber
3	avocados
2	tablespoons buttermilk
	Garlic salt (to taste)
1	bunch radish
3	tortillas per person

Trim boneless pork shoulder into 3-inch by 3-inch chunks. Remove the excess fat. Rub the pieces of pork shoulder all over with coarse sea salt. Refrigerate for at least 24 hours; 48 hours is better.

Use a cast iron enamel-coated pan. The pan needs to be large enough so that all the pork can fit inside without spilling out. Keep the pan dry and cook the pieces of pork shoulder in a single layer until very well browned. Cook as many batches as needed to keep them in a single layer. Drain the pork on a paper towel between batches. The goal is to create a thick brown crust on both the pork and the pan. Turn the pieces as little as possible so they are nice and dark before flipping them around. Once all the pork is browned, blot away any excess fat with a paper towel, then pour in about 1 cup of broth, scraping the bottom of the pan with a flat-edged utensil to release all the brown bits.

Add the pork back to the pan and heat the oven to 350 degrees. Add the orange and enough whole milk so that the pork pieces are two-thirds submerged in liquid. Add oregano, chiles, cinnamon sticks, bay leaves, ground cumin, garlic cloves, hibiscus, and peppercorns. Top the roast with banana leaves that have been soaked for 10 minutes in water.

Braise in the oven uncovered for 3½ hours, turning the pork a few times during cooking, until much of the liquid is evaporated and the pork is falling apart. Remove the pan from the oven and lift the pork pieces out of the liquid. Allow the pork to cool, then shred using a fork or put into a stand mixer with the paddle attachment.

(continued)

Serve with a cooling cucumber garnish, sliced radish, and fresh tortillas. Peel, seed, and dice a cucumber. Puree avocados in a food processor. Add cucumbers and buttermilk and puree. Add garlic salt, orange juice, and pepper to taste. Thinly slice radishes and float in ice water until serving. Wet a pan lightly with oil and warm both sides of tortillas before serving.

Beer Pairing

To enjoy the floral aroma and deep roasty flavor of the pork, pair this dish with Amber Ale. Anderson Valley's Summer Solstice (5% ABV/4 IBU) is copper in color and smooth with hints of cedar, vanilla, and pineapple on the nose and offers a light smokiness, easy hop balance, and a tinge of nut on the nose. Offer in a tulip glass.

BAKED TROUT

This recipe and pairing is perfect for a summer camping trip, a light summer dinner, or to cook over a bonfire after fishing.

- 1 **trout per person**
- 1 **bunch mint leaves**
- 2 **citrus rinds**
  Salt and pepper

Catch or select the trout. If purchasing from the store, request that the fish is gutted but retain the tail and head to keep the meat from drying where those parts are cut. If catching the trout, slice open from jaw to tail on the belly. Hook a finger into the bottom jaw and pull toward the tail to remove the innards. Run the stream or a hose through the fish to clean any stray parts from the meat.

Stuff the trout. Open the trout like a book with the scale side as the cover and back. With the inside meat facing up, sprinkle both sides with salt and pepper and stuff with the peel of orange and lemon citrus and mint leaves. If desired, the outside of the trout can be wrapped in bacon.

Cook the trout. If baking in the oven, cook at 350 degrees for 12 to 15 minutes on a baking sheet. If wrapped in bacon, plan for an extra 3 to 5 minutes and bake on a sheet that has sides. The meat will be flakey when done. If cooking over a fire, use a wire fish cooker to hold over the direct flame, flipping from side to side often until cooked (5 to 7 minutes depending on the heat from your fire) or wrap completely in foil and place into the coals at the base of the flame until cooked.

(continued)

Beer Pairing

Pair this fish with Anchor Brewing's Summer Wheat (4.5% ABV). With a heavy straw nose and lemon, wheat body, this brew is easy to drink, is crisp, and finishes quickly, like the small trout. Fresh trout will have a slightly grassy flavor to them, which is accented by the thick wheat body of the brew.

ROASTED BEETS
AND THEIR GREENS

The beet green is an underused ingredient. In late summer, these greens are bright, peppery, and much more tender than arugula. To use the green, cut it off at the base of the beet and float the green in a sink filled with cold water. The heavy dirt will sink to the bottom and the greens will float to the top. Dry the greens and tear or cut into ribbons.

4 beets (omit tough stems) and their greens
2 tablespoons extra-virgin olive oil
1 tablespoon honey
1 tablespoon balsamic vinegar
  Salt and pepper
¼ cup raw pistachios
2 tablespoons goat cheese

Peel the beets and slice into rings. Coat the slices with olive oil, balsamic, honey, salt, and pepper. Select an aged, thick, syrupy, fruity balsamic. This will be the predominant flavor in the dish. Roast at 400 degrees in a single layer until fork tender. Toss the greens with olive oil and place on top the last 5 minutes of cooking. While the beets are still warm, drizzle with more balsamic and top with raw pistachios and hunks of goat cheese.

(continued)

Beer Pairing

Pair these beets with a summery farmhouse-style ale in a tulip glass. North Coast Brewing Company's Le Merle Belgian Style Farmhouse Ale (7.9% ABV/26 IBU) has a tropical fruit note on the nose, a sweet effervescent taste, and a refreshing wheaty mouthfeel.

LOBSTER AND HOMEMADE BUTTER

Ending a summer day spent on the water with sweet, charred, grilled lobster dripping with fragrant butter, paired with a cold beer, is absolutely decadent. Catch or select a lobster that is alive and active. When the lobster is lifted, the tail should curl under and the body should move from side to side. Store the lobster on ice on the way home and in the refrigerator or cooler until cooking. Unless a fish tank with proper aeration is available, do not submerge the lobster in water until cooking or it will suffocate. Cook the lobster the day it is purchased.

1   **lobster per person**
    Pint of heavy cream

Boil the lobster whole in salted, boiling water until it turns bright red. Cooking time will vary by weight. Remove the lobster and drop into a bath of ice water to cool. Once the shell is cold enough to handle, remove the claws and tail. To remove the tail meat, just twist it off. Cut the shell off down the middle using kitchen shears and remove the tail whole. Reserve the shells. Cut the shell of the claws but leave the meat inside. Adventurous eaters may choose to reserve the green internal portion of the lobster for soups and crab cakes and to dig through the legs for additional sweet lobster meat.

The quality of homemade butter will be determined by the quality of the cream used in its creation. Select an organic cream that has not been ultrapasteurized. Pour heavy cream into an electric mixer and whisk on medium. A hand mixer can be used as well. Cover the top with

(continued)

plastic wrap. As the cream starts looking whipped, it will begin to hold peaks and dips rather than acting as a liquid. Stop the mixer, scrape the sides off the bowl to recombine, and turn the mixer on to medium speed again. Recover with plastic wrap. The cream will thicken and then turn pale yellow after about 7 minutes.

Continue to mix until it looks pebbly and the buttermilk separates from the cream. There may be an explosion as the liquid and solid separate. Stop the mixer and strain over a bowl using a strainer. Knead the butter to drain the rest of the buttermilk. Reserve the buttermilk in the fridge for dressings or fried chicken. Move the butter to a cutting board and knead until creamy.

Warm the grill. Melt the butter. Brush the grill and the lobster tail meat, tail shells, and claws with butter. When the grill is hot enough that the butter smokes, place the tail meat, tail shell, and claws on the grill. Leave only until the lobster has grill marks and is warmed through. Present the lobster tail meat on the tail shell and the claws in their shells. Offer extra melted butter for dipping.

Basics for beer: hops vines, hops, wheat (rear), and barley.

Spring pickles (spring).
Photo by Karyn Medina.

Rosemary roasted fingerlings
(spring). Photo by Karyn Medina.

Cajun shrimp (summer). Photo by Karyn Medina.

Stuffed trout (summer). Photo by Karyn Medina.

Beets, lavender, and cheese (summer). Photo by Karyn Medina.

Cutting an artichoke (fall). Photo by Karyn Medina.

Gnocchi with chorizo (fall).
Photo by Karyn Medina.

Pork Loin (fall). Photo by Karyn Medina.

Bacon jam, blue cheese, and berries (fall). Photo by Karyn Medina.

Romantic beer and chocolate pairing (winter). Photo by Karyn Medina.

(Left to right) Lambic with aged cheddar and rose smoked almonds/Blonde with provolone, mango, and cilantro/Pilsner with goat's cheese, peppercorns, and lemon/Saison with drunken goat cheese, radish, olive, and pickle (beer and cheese pairing). Photo by Karyn Medina.

(Left to right) Barleywine with blue cheese, figs, and candied nuts/Stout with ricotta, lavender honey, and chocolate/Porter with bacon and Gouda (beer and cheese pairing). Photo by Karyn Medina.

*(Left to right) Brown with figs, La Tur, and pomegranate/Pale with moz-
zarella, cilantro, red onion, beet horseradish, and mango/Red with chives,
apples, and cheddar pub cheese/IPA with cheddar, fennel, and Aleppo (beer
and cheese pairing). Photo by Karyn Medina.*

Beer Pairing

To pair this butter and lobster with a chili beer, select Ballast Point Brewing's Abandon Ship Chipotle Chile in a pint glass (7% ABV/32 IBU). This beer is balanced with a mix between tart and lingering smoke with a chile bite in the back of the throat. This will highlight the sweet, juicy, and grilled flavors in the lobster. Add ½ teaspoon cinnamon, 3 tablespoons fresh chopped parsley, and 1 teaspoon lemon juice to the butter to maximize the pairing.

To pair this dish with a floral brew, select Upright Brewing's Flora Rustica Belgian-style Saison (5.1% ABV/18 IBU). Steep the cream with ½ cup dried hibiscus and chamomile tea over low heat before making butter. Strain and chill the cream before whipping it into butter. This pairing will accentuate flavors of fresh pear, marigolds, and salty sweetness in the lobster. Serve in a tulip glass

To pair this dish with a blonde ale, select Firestone Walker Brewing's Solace (4.8% ABU/13 IBU). Mix the butter with the leaves of 1 bunch fresh tarragon, ½ bunch fresh chives, 1 tablespoon fresh parsley, and citrus zest. This pairing will highlight flavors of nutmeg and cloves on the beer nose while creating a decadent, herbal flavor in the butter.

PORK MEATBALLS

A meatloaf mix traditionally features three meats: veal, pork, and beef. We do not advocate eating veal as the calf has been restrained to a cage with limited movement for a very short life. Instead, this recipe uses pork in the form of bacon, prosciutto, and Italian sausage.

1	pound sweet Italian sausage
¼	pound bacon, diced
¼	cup white onion, chopped
⅛	cup shredded Parmesan cheese
3	tablespoons golden raisins
2	tablespoons cilantro, chopped
¼	cup panko bread crumbs
1	egg
¾	pound prosciutto

Combine sausage with bacon in a bowl. Add finely chopped onion, Parmesan cheese, chopped golden raisins, chopped cilantro, panko bread crumbs, and the egg. Mix until combined. Flatten a large spoonful of the meat mixture into a palm and add a chunk of prosciutto in the middle. Form a meatball around the outside of the prosciutto. Bake the meatballs in a single layer without touching at 425 degrees until 140 degrees inside.

Beer Pairing

Pair this dish with an aged wheat beer in a snifter. Allagash Brewing's Odyssey (10.4% ABV/30 IBU) is a dark wheat beer that is aged in oak barrels. Expect a thicker mouthfeel, a slight coating sensation on the tongue, and a fragrant lingering taste. The saltiness of the bacon and the cured meat will shine through. This pairing will create flavors of raisin, dates, coffee, and vanilla.

Also consider pairing this dish with a complex Farmhouse ale like Pepe Nero by Goose Island Brewery in a tulip glass (6% ABV/30 IBU). This beer offers a peppery aroma with licorice spices that will accent the spices in the Italian sausage. Expect a creamy finish that will oppose the savory meat flavors and a coffee aroma that will deepen the saltiness of the meat.

CANTALOUPE CRÈME BRÛLÉE

1 quart fresh organic heavy cream
1 vanilla bean (do not substitute with vanilla extract)
2 large, peeled slices cantaloupe
½ cup sugar plus ½ cup sugar
6 eggs, yolks only

Preheat the oven to 325 degrees. Slice the vanilla bean down the middle vertically. Scrape the inside pulp out with a spoon. Place cream and vanilla bean and its pulp into a medium saucepan set over medium-high heat and bring to a boil. Do not burn the cream. Remove from the heat, add cantaloupe, and cover and allow to sit for 15 minutes. Pour through a strainer to remove the melon and vanilla bean.

In a medium bowl, whisk together ½ cup sugar and egg yolks until well blended. Add the cream a little at a time, stirring continually so the eggs don't cook and scramble. Pour the liquid into ramekins. Place the ramekins into a large cake pan or roasting pan. Pour enough hot water into the pan to come halfway up the sides of the ramekins. Bake just until the crème brûlée is set, but still trembling in the center, approximately 40 to 45 minutes. Remove the ramekins from the roasting pan and refrigerate for at least 2 hours (up to 3 days if necessary).

Remove the crème brûlée from the refrigerator for at least 30 minutes. Divide ½ cup sugar equally among the dishes and spread evenly on top. Using a torch, melt the sugar and form a crispy top. Allow the crème brûlée to sit for at least 5 minutes before serving. Serve with fresh melon slices.

Beer Pairing

Pair this dish with a Farmhouse-style brew or an oatmeal stout. Goose Island Brewing's Sofie is a Belgian-style Farmhouse Ale (6.5% ABV/25 IBU). While the crème brûlée offers a creamy texture and mouth-watering fruit flavor, this brew adds a white pepper aroma that contrasts with the fruit and a pungent vanilla flavor that brings a velvet nature to the cream. Serve in a tulip glass.

For a decadent oatmeal cookie experience, pair this dish with Firestone Walker Brewing's Velvet Merlin Oatmeal Stout (5.5% ABV/30 IBU). This brew has a smooth, creamy, and chocolaty offering, an exact balance for the fruity cream. This pairing tastes of burned marshmallows and campfire. Serve in a pinot glass.

CHAPTER 5

Fall

Leaves are falling, heat is waning, and cool nights invite heartier foods in fall. Yeasty, salty, fatty, nutty, and overripe flavors are present this time of year in both food and beer. These flavors bridge the gap between winter's hearty, roasty, meaty, starchy, earthy flavors to summer's grilled, fruity, ripe, pungent, and herbal flavors. The weather dictates an indoor/outdoor cooking experience. Foods range from Oktoberfest sausages on the grill to decadent drippy fondue inside on the stove.

Fall beer flavors are the jazz saxophone of the orchestra; sultry and seductive in their rich red hues, melodic without being repetitive. Fall beers have a maltier, or thicker, mouthfeel than a light summer beer. Fall brews begin the slow transition into winter's syrupy dark brews by tanning their color and increasing their alcohol content. Where spring and summer brews are thin, creamy, and effervescent in texture, the beers of fall are silky with a higher alcohol presence. Where winter beers rely on booming drums with darker malts and result in thick, coating textures, fall beers use hops to produce citric and lively characters, hidden in smooth red liquid.

Märzen and Brown are fall beers. Märzen is German for "March," named after the month when it was brewed. This lager was traditionally cold stored all summer and opened in the fall to celebrate the harvest. This Oktoberfest style holds a darker ruby color because of the variety of barley malts used. With names like Moravian and Carmel, these malts sweeten as well as darken the brew. Smoke, aged cheese, apple, even chestnut flavors are prevalent in this type of beer.

Brown ales originated from northern England and were the predominant style before advances in malting occurred. Browns are warmer fermented at room temperatures, making them easy to brew in the summer and to open in the fall, and they lend flavors like light chocolate, toffee, and ripe fruit.

BLACKENED ARTICHOKES WITH SESAME DIPPING SAUCE

One of the more common artichokes is the large, round globe artichoke. Heirloom varieties are available and can be the same shape as a globe but are sold much smaller and sometimes are misnamed baby artichokes, or come in elongated shapes, more similar in shape and size to an avocado. Artichokes are often steamed or boiled whole, then their leaves are pulled back and the meat scrapped off the base of each leaf with the teeth. The interior of an artichoke is filled with tiny hairs that cover the sweet, dense meat found in the heart. Artichokes grow on a tall stalk and the hairs eventually bloom into purple flowers.

> Artichokes (1 per person)
> ¼   cup sesame oil
> 4   tablespoons honey
> 3   tablespoons lemon juice
> 1   cup mayonnaise
> ⅛   cup chopped parsley
>   Few dashes steak sauce
>   Pinch of salt
>   Extra-virgin olive oil, for drizzling, or butter

This recipe requires that the artichoke be cleaned of thistles, steamed, then grilled. Prepare a bowl of ice water with lemon juice to prevent the cut areas of the artichoke from browning. Trim the base of the stem just slightly and remove any hard and dark area. Use a serrated knife and cut the artichoke vertically up the middle of the choke from the base of the

(continued)

stem to the tip of the leaves. Place the flat side of the chokes down on the cutting surface and cut in half vertically again. Now that the choke is divided in quarters, each quarter has an almost equal ratio of stem, leaves, and thistles. Turn all quarters, thistle side facing up, and use a small paring knife to cut horizontally along the base of the thistle back to the base of the hearty leaves. Do not cut all the way through; the goal is to end up with a chair-shaped cut rather than a backless barstool, meaning that the thistle is removed but the stem, heart, and hearty green leaves are still attached as one piece. After cutting along the base, grab the soft, lightly colored leaves near the thistle and pull away from the dark hearty leaves. Rinse the last of the thistles away under running water and then float in the lemon ice water while trimming continues.

Lay the trimmed artichoke quarters in a single layer on their sides in a steam basket and steam over boiling water until the heart is fork tender, about 15 minutes. Boiling is an option; however, the chokes can taste waterlogged, even after the blackening process, which eliminates the hint of sweet umami that pairs so delicately with fall brews. After steaming, drizzle with olive oil or melted butter.

While the chokes steam, heat the grill or grill pan until it smokes when oil is on the grill, or heat the broiler to 475 degrees. Make a dipping sauce (serves 6) that offers sweet, salty, savory, and spicy flavors. Mix the sesame oil, honey, lemon juice, mayonnaise, parsley, Worcestershire or A-1 sauce, and salt. Store on ice or in the fridge to thicken up. Grill the artichokes on all sides for about 5 minutes until black and crispy on the edges or broil about 3 minutes.

Beer Pairing

Pair the grilled artichokes with a Märzen. Categorically, Märzens are brewed in March and stored until Oktoberfest. This pairing is balanced and generates a nutty, charred flavor. Sudwerk Brewery's Marzen (5.3% ABV) offers a moderate sweetness with a moderate bitterness. Expect a caramel and fruity nose that will highlight the honey in the dipping sauce. Offer a pint glass.

PIZZA AND TOMATO SAUCE

A beer and food pairing book is not complete without discussing pizza and beer. However, this is not an obligatory reference; the following artisan recipe will produce four simple fresh pizzas reminiscent of wood-fired Italian pizza.

DOUGH

1½ cups warm water
½ teaspoon active dry yeast
4 cups all-purpose flour
1 teaspoon salt
1 teaspoon sugar
1 teaspoon baking soda

To create pizza dough, mix warm water (105 degrees) with dry yeast. Let the mixture stand for at least 10 minutes to proof. Gradually pour 2 cups of all-purpose flour onto the mixture and stir to combine. Once all ingredients are combined, mix for about 1 minute to form a sponge. Cover the mixture with a towel and let it rest for 1 hour, outside the fridge. Add salt, sugar, and baking soda. Then add 2 more cups all-purpose flour, ½ cup at a time, mixing to create dough. Remove the mixture from the bowl and store in a clean, oiled bowl overnight, covered by a kitchen towel.

Divide the dough into 4 balls and let rise again under a wet kitchen towel in the fridge for at least 1 hour and up to 3 days. Roll out and top with tomato sauce.

TOMATO SAUCE

- 2 pounds tomatoes
- 1 clove chopped garlic
- 4 tablespoons olive oil
- 1 bay leaf
  Handful chopped fresh basil
- 1 tablespoon savory
- 1 tablespoon oregano
  Mild white cheese

Turn summer's overripe tomatoes into sauce early in the fall. Score the tomato skin where the stem has been removed from the tomato with an x shape. Drop the tomato into boiling water for 10 seconds then into ice water. The edges of the x will lift up. Over a large skillet, grab the corners of the x and peel the skin from the tomato. Catch all pulp, seeds, and juices into the skillet. Warm the skillet over medium heat. Add chopped garlic, olive oil, bay leaf, basil, savory, and oregano. Stir frequently and cook for about 10 minutes until the juices are bubbling and reducing. Add salt and pepper and remove the bay leaf. Remove from heat. If a smooth sauce is desired, use a blender or immersion blender to smooth. Spread on the dough and top with a mild white cheese.

Preheat the oven to 475 degrees. Bake the pizza on a screen or a baking sheet for 15 minutes in a convection oven, 20 minutes in a standard oven.

(continued)

Beer Pairing

Pair acidic tomato and yeasty bread with hoppy pale ales. Oskar Blues Brewing's Dales Pale Ale (6.5% ABV/65 IBU) pairs well with high IBU and citric hops. Stored in a can, this beer offers a fresh, bright, hoppy nose even after long storage. The savory and oregano blend well with the bold spice of the beer. Expect a soft texture in the mouth, despite the high spices in both the food and the beer. Spice flavors will extend down the throat and produce a refreshing burn. Offer a pint glass.

CURING BACON AND BACON JAM

Making homemade, nitrate-free bacon is so simple and much more flavorful and healthful than commercially processed bacon. Work with a butcher from a noncommercial grocery, a high-end grocery chain, an Asian grocery or directly with a pork farmer to purchase pork belly. This cut is usually sold in 3- to 12-pound increments. Purchase as much as you would like, knowing that bacon freezes well. Ask that the skin remain on the belly, as a tool for curing later. Do not purchase any pieces smaller than 2 pounds.

BACON

½   cup kosher sea salt

3–5   pounds pork belly

      Assorted spices (see below)

2   cups wood chips

Gather kosher sea salt, large glass baking dishes, and plastic wrap. Place the belly skin side down in the glass container. Cut the belly into 3- to 5-pound increments so they fit into the glass containers. Do not use metal or plastic for this process as the salts can leach bacteria from the plastic and metallic properties from the metal into the meat. Sprinkle a handful of kosher salt onto the sides and top of the belly to begin pulling moisture out of the meat into the salt. There is no point in salting the skin side; the skin of the pig is thick like tire tread. The salt will quickly appear to absorb into the meat. What is actually happening is that moisture is com-

(continued)

ing to the top of the meat and the salt is draining the moisture through the large salt grains into the pan. This is a great time to add flavoring agents to the top of the salt so it can push the flavor into the meat as the moisture leaves. Quantities are not exact in the combinations that follow; we suggest adding these ingredients in 2-tablespoon increments until coated. For Asian herbal bacon, combine rosemary, peppercorns, pomegranate seeds, bay leaf, juniper berry, liquid smoke, and Hoisin sauce along the top of the belly. For a breakfast blend, combine liquid smoke, cinnamon, maple syrup, and peppercorns. For a spicy bacon, combine dried peppers, fresh garlic, mustard powder, hot sauce, and citrus peel.

Tightly cover the belly and store in the fridge for 3 to 5 days. The salt will disappear and a large puddle of liquid will develop. The liquid can be drained daily to make firmer bacon but is not necessary. If another glass container is placed on top of the bacon with something heavy on the top like jars, cans, or a six pack of beer, the belly will release more liquid, making much firmer bacon.

To smoke the belly in a smoker, follow the directions in your smoker. To infuse a smoke flavor in the belly in your oven, soak wood chips in enough liquid to cover them for at least 20 minutes. Wine or high-sugar fruit juice works best. Add the moist chips and their liquid to a glass baking dish larger than the piece of belly and place a wire rack above the dish. Place the belly *skin side up* on the wire rack above the wood chips so that the flesh side of the belly faces the chips. Cook in the oven at 225 degrees until the internal temperature of the belly reaches at least 150 degrees.

BACON JAM

- 2 large white onions
- 4 cloves garlic
- 1 teaspoon instant espresso
- ½ cup maple syrup
- ¼ cup brown sugar
- ¼ cup apple cider vinegar
  Few dashes steak sauce
  Few dashes hot sauce
- 1 cup water

To make bacon jam, allow the smoked belly to cool. Remove about 1 pound of bacon and dice. In a skillet, cook over medium heat until browned but still very pliable. Remove from the heat and place into a large saucepan. Slice white onions and garlic and brown in the bacon fat in the skillet. Add to the saucepan the instant espresso, maple syrup, brown sugar, vinegar, a few dashes of Worcestershire or A-1 sauce, a few dashes of hot sauce, and 1 cup of water. Let simmer over low heat for 3 hours, adding water as needed.

Serve on crusty bread with gorgonzola and berries or stuffed in raviolis with a cream sauce.

(*continued*)

Beer Pairing

Pair with a complex brew, such as a Saison or fruit vegetable beer. Goose Island Brewing's Pepe Nero (6.4% ABV/30 IBU) adds a complex nuttiness to the jam. Roasted chestnut aroma, mahogany color, and peppercorn flavor mimic the meaty jam but the saison extends the complexity of the jam with the addition of a grounding earthy flavor. Offer in a pint glass. The Bruery's Autumn Maple (10% ABV/25 IBU) is brewed with yams and offers a nose of cinnamon, nutmeg, and other fall spices. Paired with the bacon jam, this becomes an elegant Thanksgiving appetizer. Offer in a snifter.

HOME-CURED SALMON

Salmon swim upstream in the fall, making them more available to catch wild in rivers. If catching wild salmon is not an option, select salmon based on sustainable seafood lists. Curing salmon, by definition, means to use salt and age to decrease moisture and impart flavor.

Side of salmon, skin intact
4 ounces sea salt (per pound of salmon)
6 ounces white sugar (per pound of salmon)
6 ounces brown sugar
2 teaspoons ground pepper
Curing spices (as noted below, for desired flavor)
½ cup jasmine rice
¼ cup brown sugar
1 citrus peel

To cure salmon, use a similar technique to that in the previous bacon recipe. Place a side of salmon skin side down in a glass dish. In a separate bowl, per pound of salmon, combine sea salt or kosher salt with white sugar, brown sugar, and ground pepper. Pack the curing solution onto the top of the salmon and add herbs, liquid, and citrus. For a bright salmon, combine a handful of lemon zest and dill fronds with ¼ cup of vermouth and drizzle on the salmon. For a lingering smoky flavor, combine fennel bulb, toasted fennel seeds, liquid smoke, and ¼ cup orange juice. For a salty briny salmon, combine capers, lemon zest, red onion, and

(continued)

¼ cup champagne vinegar. Cover tightly with plastic wrap and place a heavy weight on top. Refrigerate until the thickest part feels firm to the touch, at least 48 hours, more likely 3 to 4 days. Discard the spices and rinse dry.

Bring a gas grill to a medium-high heat. Make a square of foil that is at least four layers thick and make a pile of jasmine rice, brown sugar, and the peel of citrus. Place the flavoring package onto the gas grill grate and cook the salmon, skin side down, for about 5 minutes to add a smoky flavor and firm the texture.

Beer Pairing

Pair cured salmon with a Belgian-style double in a tulip glass. Expect this pairing to balance the smoky flavor of the fish with heavy herbal flavors of bay, lemongrass, and coriander. Uncommon Brewers' Siamese Twin Ale (8.5% ABV/25 IBU) offers a floral, herbal nose with a pepper lime bite. With this pairing, the tender fish flavor, smoky grill flavor, and herbal beer flavor will synchronize. Consider echoing the smooth, creamy mouthfeel of the beer with a spreadable cream cheese or soft brown bread.

OKTOBERFEST PRETZELS AND SMOKED GOUDA SAUCE

——————————————————————————————————————— ᘒꙅ

L arge, soft pretzels with cheese sauce make an excellent appetizer before a meal of sausage and kraut.

4½   cup all-purpose flour (divided)
2   cups whole milk
2   cups Gouda
1   teaspoon cayenne
4   cups 110-degree water
1   tablespoon sugar
3   teaspoons salt
1   package active dry yeast
4   cups all-purpose flour
2   tablespoons melted butter
2   tablespoons baking soda
    Salt and pepper to taste

Add ½ cup all-purpose flour to a saucepan over medium heat and slowly whisk in whole milk. Select an aged, smoked Gouda cheese. Look for small textural differences within each part of the cheese from softer to firm with crystals and smoky flavor. Grate cheese and combine with the milky flour. Add fresh cracked pepper and cayenne.

For slightly sour pretzels, let the dough proof at room temperature for at least 24 hours. Combine 1⅓ cups 110-degree water with sugar and salt. Stir until dissolved and add yeast. Wait until the mixture foams, less

(continued)

than 10 minutes, and add 4 cups flour and melted butter. Mix with a wooden spoon until combined. Using a dough hook in a stand mixer, mix on medium high until the dough is smooth. Cover with plastic wrap and place into a cold oven with the light on for 2 hours. Pull it out from the oven. Knead the dough and store it covered in a moist kitchen towel for at least 24 hours. Knead the dough again.

Preheat the oven to 450 degrees and bring 8 cups water and baking soda to a boil. Shape the dough into twists and toss into the water for about 30 seconds. Place on a nonstick baking sheet, sprinkle with salt, and bake for 12 minutes. Serve with sauce.

Beer Pairing

The smoky aged cheese and yeasty sour pretzels highlight the roasted flavors of fall beers like Pyramid Brewing's Oktoberfest or New Belgium's Red Hoptober. Both contribute a darker caramel flavor as well as pronounced hop bite to hold up to the cheese. Serve in an Oktoberfest 1-liter glass or ceramic mug.

OKTOBERFEST KRAUT AND SAUSAGE

Sauerkraut is a fermented cabbage that is often served with sausages. During the fermentation process, mold on the top of the leaves is normal.

4 pounds cabbage
2 tablespoons pickling salt
1 teaspoon sugar
3 tablespoons crushed juniper berries

To make sauerkraut that pairs well with Oktoberfest-style brews, gather fresh, crispy cabbage. Remove and reserve the outer layer of leaves and cut the cabbage in half. Remove the core and cut the cabbage into long strips no wider than a quarter. Mix pickling salt with sugar and crushed juniper berries. Place the cabbage in a large glass bowl and rub the sugar-salt-juniper mixture throughout the cabbage until the cabbage begins to appear wet all over.

Pickling salt is important to use because it maintains anti-caking properties for the several weeks the cabbage will ferment. Sea salt or table salt can build up, dry, and fall off the cabbage. If this happens, the cabbage will rot rather than ferment. Pack the cabbage into sanitized Mason glass jars with a two-part lid and place one of the previously removed exterior leaves on the very top. Close tightly and store in a cool, dark area for 24 hours. Check the cabbage, looking for liquid brine with tiny bubbles developing. If the cabbage is not fully covered in its own brine within 48 hours, mix 1 ½ tablespoons of pickling salt into

(continued)

1 quart water and fill the jars. Continue storing at 55–65 degrees for 5 weeks. Serve with sausage and mustard.

Beer Pairing

True to theme, pair this recipe with an Oktoberfest lager. Boston Beer's Oktoberfest lager (5.3% ABV/15 IBU) is an excellent representation of an American Oktoberfest beer. This beer features a malty sweetness, shallow hop character, and an aroma of baking bread. The beer extends the juicy sausage flavor and allows the kraut to appear ripe rather than sour. Serve in a mug.

PORK LOIN WITH CELERY LEAF AND GREEN PEPPERCORN CREAM

The quintessential harvest meal, roasted pork loin, is brined and served with tangy celery sauce to pair with slightly sour beers. Brining means to soak a meat in a salted water to plump up the muscle fibers for moist meat. The loin or tenderloin cuts can be used for this recipe.

> Pork loin brined in sea salt (per weight of loin as
> outlined below), ⅓–½ pound per person
> ¼ cup combined chopped celery, chestnuts, and
> cremini mushrooms (per 2 pounds of pork)
> ½ cup paired beer
> 1 cup chopped celery leaves, plus extra for garnish
> 1 tablespoon Dijon mustard
> 1 teaspoon green peppercorns
> ⅛ cup cream

Source an antibiotic-free pork loin. Debone the loin. Brine the loin for 4 hours in the refrigerator in a ratio of ¼ cup sea salt to 1 gallon of water (per 2 people). Rinse clean and open the loin flat on a cutting surface. Stuff the interior with combined chopped celery, chestnuts, and cremini mushrooms. The celery will perfume the roast and provide a slightly sour flavor. The mushrooms and chestnuts will combine with the juices of the pork and almost dissolve into the celery. Using kitchen twine, roll the loin onto itself and tie with twine. Cover the exterior with sage and bacon. Bake at 350 degrees until the interior comes to 120 degrees, remove the sage and bacon,

(continued)

and continue cooking until the interior comes to 140 degrees. Remove the loin from the baking tray, remove the string, and let it rest.

Place the baking tray on the stove over medium heat and scrape the burned bits off the bottom. Add ½ cup of the beer that is being paired and bring to a simmer until the liquid is reduced by half. Add 1 cup of chopped celery leaves. Continue to simmer. Add Dijon mustard, green peppercorns, and cream. Remove from heat. Slice the loin and pour the sauce on top. Garnish with fresh celery leaves.

Beer Pairing

Allagash Brewing's Curieux (11% ABV/28 IBU) is a bourbon barrel-aged strong ale. The velvety soft mouthfeel highlights the briny pork juices and a coconut nose is an exceptional counterbalance to the celery. Sour, ripe, and vanilla flavors allow the cream sauce to shine as a silky coat over the entire mouth. Serve in a snifter.

Bear Republic's Red Rocket Ale (6.8% ABV/67 IBU) offers an alternative approach to pairing. A Scottish-style red ale, this beer creates a soft background for the celery and peppercorns to shine as a pungent, sour sauce. The recipe offers little sweetness outside the flavor of the pork and the Red Rocket fills this void with creamy, sweet notes. Serve in a pint glass.

GNOCCHI IN CHORIZO-SAGE BROWN BUTTER

Gnocchi is a potato pasta. Gnocchi is often made by boiling a white russet potato, removing the skin, and pushing the interior through a ricer, then mixing with egg to form a paste that is shaped into small dumplings and boiled until the pasta floats. Here, sweet potato is used and requires baking rather than boiling to maintain the integrity of the dumpling.

1½	pounds sweet potatoes
1	cup fresh ricotta
⅛	cup fresh sage, chopped, plus extra for garnish
½	cup Parmesan cheese
3	tablespoons brown sugar
1	tablespoon salt
1	teaspoon nutmeg
	All-purpose flour
½	cup chorizo
1	stick butter

Rinse, peel, dry, and pierce sweet potatoes with a fork. Microwave for 10 minutes until tender on the inside, then cool and chop into small pieces. Place potatoes in a food processor with fresh ricotta, sage, Parmesan cheese, brown sugar, salt, and nutmeg. Pulse until mixed.

Make a pile of flour on a clean, dry work surface. Using as much flour as needed, form the gnocchi mix from the consistency of sticky play dough into long, thin, flour-coated logs. Several cups of flour may be

(continued)

needed. Chop the logs into bite-sized pieces. Roll the small pieces off the back of a fork or gnocchi board to create indentations in the dumpling that will hold sauce. Bake on a nonstick cookie sheet at 325 degrees for 10 minutes. While baking, brown chorizo in a skillet until crispy and drain. Melt butter in the same pan, add a handful of fresh chopped sage, and turn up heat until the butter browns and bubbles. Combine the butter and chorizo and toss over gnocchi.

Beer Pairing

Pair this dish with a low-IBU, sweet and roasty ale. Lagunitas Brewing's Wilco Tango Foxtrot Brown Ale (7.8 ABV/64 IBU) mimics the brown color of the dish and echoes similar flavors with hops to highlight the chorizo, a silky mouthfeel to celebrate the tender sweet potato, and a slightly herbal nose to highlight the sage. Offer in a mug.

PASTA AND
WHITE FALL LASAGNA

Perfect for late fall as the weather is cold more often than it is cool, this lasagna is warming, pairs perfectly with Weiss or wheat beers, and allows for any late fall and early winter vegetables to be used. The key is roasting the produce until it is fork-tender before adding to the lasagna so the lasagna can form into thin layers, more like a pastry than pasta. No-bake noodles can be used for this recipe or make your own pasta and dry it overnight before using.

4	cups all-purpose flour
6	eggs
2	tablespoons plus 4 tablespoons olive oil
2	cups winter veggies: eggplant, squash, broccoli rabe, bell peppers, and chard
2	cloves garlic
3	tablespoons butter
¼	cup flour
1	cup cream
2	cups milk
1	cup white cheese (mozzarella or fontina)
½	cup Parmesan cheese
2	tablespoons fresh chopped herbs such as parsley, oregano, or thyme

To make pasta dough by hand, pour 4 cups of flour onto a clean, dry work surface in a big mound. Form a well in the middle of the mound,

(*continued*)

and one at a time, add up to 6 room-temperature eggs in the well. Add 2 tablespoons of olive oil. After adding each egg, stir with either your fingers or a fork to whisk the eggs and begin integrating the flour into the wet mixture. Slowly fold the sides of the mound into the center until all wet and dry ingredients are fully integrated. The final consistency should be moist, but not sticky, and fully mixed. Starting on the highest setting of a pasta machine, begin feeding the pasta through, reducing the setting each time until the pasta is almost see-through. Cut the pasta into strips the length of the baking dish. Allow it to dry overnight.

Use a mixture of winter squash, broccoli rabe, eggplant, bell peppers, and chard. Thinly slice and coat veggies in 4 tablespoons of olive oil, salt, and pepper and roast in the oven in a single layer at 400 degrees until tender, about 20 minutes. Remove and turn oven up to 425 degrees.

Chop garlic and cook in a saucepan in butter over medium heat until fragrant, which will take less than 1 minute. Prepare ¼ cup of flour, cream, and milk. Using a whisk, add flour, 1 tablespoon at a time to the saucepan, whisking until it is coated in butter before adding more. Complete this step quickly; take less than 2 minutes total to add flour, whisk, and coat it, and add more flour until all the flour has been added. Add the milk, then the cream, whisking constantly. Turn the heat to medium low and whisk for 8 minutes. Remove from heat. Add freshly grated nutmeg, white cheese (mozzarella or fontina), and Parmesan cheese. Add fresh chopped herbs such as parsley, oregano, or thyme.

Layer the pasta, then veggies and a bit of ricotta, then noodles, then white cheesy sauce, then noodles, then veggies with ricotta, then noodles, then sauce. Top with additional grated cheese and nutmeg and bake covered until bubbling. Uncover for 5 minutes to brown top. Let stand 10 minutes, then serve.

Beer Pairing

Amond and floral flavors complement the creamy flavor of this dish. Pair Boston Beer's Cherry Wheat beer (5.3% ABV/23 IBU) with the lasagna, especially if it contains squash. This beer has an almond blossom nose that highlights the sweet flavor of cooked cream but counterbalances with a stinging mouthfeel that cleanses the palate. Offer in a tulip glass.

The Bruery's Hottenroth Berliner Weiss (3.1% ABV/2 IBU) pairs well with ripe vegetable fillings such as eggplant. This German-style wheat beer offers slightly sour flavors captured during open fermentation. Where the Cherry Wheat highlights the sweet, juicy nature of the dish, the Weiss will highlight the doughy, chewy layers of the lasagna. Offer in a pint glass.

DRUNKEN CHEESE FONDUE

Fondue, like lasagna, is a dairy- and carb-heavy meal for late in the fall that highlights the bold hops and heavy malt body of fall brews. Cheese fondue is traditionally a Swiss dish, consisting of cheese, wine, and kirsch (cherry liquor).

12	ounces of cheese per person
2	tablespoons flour
1	clove garlic
1½	cups amber ale
1	teaspoon brown mustard
1	shot kirsch
	Assortment of bread, green apples, blanched broccoli, and celery to dip
	Salt and pepper to taste

Grate 12 ounces of cheese per person and allow it to come to room temperature. Try a combination of aged white cheddar, sharp Gruyère, and aged Emmenthaler. Rub the inside of a heavy saucepan with garlic. Over medium-high heat, bring amber ale and brown mustard to a steam, just before the mixture begins to bubble. Add the cheese, *one handful at a time,* stirring in a figure-eight motion until fully melted before adding the next. Continue until the sauce is thick enough to coat the back of a spoon. Add salt and pepper and a shot of cherry kirsch. Pour into a fondue pot to serve. Offer green apples, crusty bread, blanched broccoli, and celery to dip.

Beer Pairing

Various cheese flavors will become more prevalent based on the brew selection. Select an amber and increase or decrease the IBU to control the sharp flavor of the dish. Firestone Walker Brewing's Double Barrel Ale (5% ABV/30 IBU) will allow the strong, aged Emmenthaler to shine. This amber ale draws out the slight stink of the cheese with a similar hop aroma that is mustardy and oaky. Flavors of aged wood, aged cheese crystals, and celery will become pronounced. New Belgium Brewing's Fat Tire Amber Ale (5.2% ABV/18.5 IBU) will pinpoint the flavor of the cheddar cheese. This amber ale is floral and fruity with a tempered hop spice. The lower-IBU brew will contrast nicely to green apples and the fondue will become silky in texture. Offer in a pint or tulip glass.

PUMPKIN SEED BRITTLE

B rittle is a mixture of sugar and water cooked over high heat, combined with butter, then allowed to cool in a thin layer. Any nuts or seeds can be added to this recipe in place of pumpkin seeds. If dairy is added at the same time as butter, the brittle becomes a caramel.

1 quart cream
½ cup chopped fresh pumpkin or
    4 tablespoons canned pumpkin
¾ cup cane sugar
½ teaspoon ginger
¼ cup raw pumpkin seeds
⅓ cup cool water

Bring cream to a low simmer. Add chunks of fresh pumpkin or canned pumpkin. Cover the cream, turn off the heat, and let it sit for 15 minutes. Strain the pumpkin out of the cream and cool the cream completely in the refrigerator. Refer to the Lobster recipe in the Summer chapter to make pumpkin butter from the chilled cream.

Line a few plates or a baking sheet with parchment paper. In a small saucepan, mix cane sugar with ⅓ cup cool water. Cook over high heat for 5 to 7 minutes. Use a nonstick spatula to stir. Take the pan off the heat and add 1 tablespoon of pumpkin butter, a pinch of ginger, and a palm-ful of pumpkin seeds. (Use the remaining butter to sear a fall steak, sauté veggies in, or use on rustic fall bread.) Pour the brittle on the plates or parchment paper. The thinner the brittle, the quicker it will set.

Beer Pairing

Pair this brittle with Mendocino Imperial Barleywine-style Ale (11% ABV/55 IBU). This brew pours deep ruby with a lacy white head. This pairing will create flavors of dark fruit, caramel, and raisins. The silky sweetness of the brew will counteract the sweet shards of brittle. Offer in a snifter.

CHAPTER 6

Winter

Damp and cold with harvest and holiday celebrations, winter is an opportunity to hunker down and drink thick brews paired with soul-warming dishes. Hearty root vegetables, bright citrus, and tough greens thrive while all else hibernates. Big, complex, roasty, meaty, starchy, sweet, and syrupy flavors grace the table and the glass. The oven dominates food preparation with slow roasts, simmering soups, fried foods, and baking dishes.

Winter beer flavors are the booming drums, clanging brass, and slow, lingering piano notes of the symphony. The thick, booming mouthfeel of the winter brews is brought on by dark, roasted malts and higher alcohol content. Creamy in texture but spicy and biting in flavor, winter brews coat the entire mouth and swallow with a slow glug. Featuring ingredients like cocoa, cinnamon, vanilla, and smoke, the clanging brass of winter beers must be paired by equally dominant food flavors created by complex spices, dried herbs, dried fruits, pungent greens, rich seafoods, and slow roasting.

Barleywine and porters are brews of the winter. Barleywine is an ale with higher alcohol levels, more similar to a wine than a beer in ABV, but brewed like beer. In some cases, these beers are 10% ABV or higher. Designed as a celebration beer, this brew was created to satisfy British royalty when ties with southern wine-making countries were strained and was released by breweries as celebratory ales around the holidays. Expect flavors of sherry, raisins, overripe fruit, brandied nuts, and vanilla in this dessert beer.

Porters are warm fermented ales, heavy with malts. Sometimes called a sandwich in a bottle, porters were designed for the workers in the railroad industry (porters), as a way to keep them happy and working with fewer breaks. Usually garnet in color, these heavier brews pair well with the heavy meats of the holiday table, highlighting flavors of bread, dark chocolate, toffee, and roasted nuts.

SCALLOPS WITH CARAMELIZED LEEKS

Scallops are a shellfish found in saltwater. To sear a perfect scallop, ensure that the scallop is chilled but not frozen by defrosting if necessary and keeping in the refrigerator. Leeks are in the onion family. They do not grow large bulbs; instead they have a long white base with roots at the bottom and tall green stalks that spread out like a fan.

2–3	scallops per person
4	tablespoons combined, butter/olive oil
½	leek per person
	Truffle oil (for drizzling)
	Pinch salt

Pat all parts of the surface of the scallop dry with a paper towel and store on a dry, cool plate lined with another paper towel. Sear the two flat sides of the scallop on medium-high heat in an equal ratio of butter and olive oil. Use a nonstick pan and start with 2 tablespoons of butter and 2 tablespoons of olive oil. Heat on medium-high heat until the butter is hot enough to foam slightly. Salt one of the two flat sides of the scallop and place it salted side down into the foaming butter. Salt the flat side that is facing up. Do not move the scallop for at least 30 seconds so that it has time to develop a crust. Each scallop should be at least 1 inch away from the nearest scallop so that they sear, not steam. Now that the flat sides of the scallop are horizontal, the vertical sides of the scallop will be the part to watch to gauge doneness. They will be opaque and slippery;

(continued)

after 30 seconds to 1 minute (depending on thickness), the opaque will slowly turn to firm white. At that time, flip the scallop. Check for a crusty, brown top. If brown, timing was perfect. If not, turn up the heat on the next scallop. Moving the scallop around the pan tears the crust that is developing on the part of the scallop touching the pan. Leave it still again for up to another minute, then remove. Serve scallops immediately. If they sit, or sit covered, the texture will change back to slippery and the lovely brown crust will disappear.

Remove the roots and dark green tops from the leeks, cutting horizontally to retain only the midsection. Slice lengthwise in half to open the midsection, then in half again. In a sink full of cold water, float the layers of the leek to rinse the dirt away. The dirt will settle to the bottom and the leeks will remain on the top.

Melt butter in a large frying pan over medium-low heat. Finely chop the leeks and add to the melted butter. Add a dash of olive oil or a spoonful of duck or bacon fat as well. Turn the heat to medium and allow the leeks to caramelize. Stir the leeks to coat them in fat and add a pinch of salt. Stir regularly until the leeks are brown and mushy. When leeks are caramelized, remove from pan. Wait until right before serving and sear scallop. Present cooked scallops on a bed of smeared leeks. Drizzle with truffle oil.

Beer Pairing

Pair seared scallops with a wit or white beer with champagne characteristics. High effervescence will complement the silky texture of the scallop. The light, slightly sour, yeasty nose will be anchored by the caramelized leeks. Truffle oil is earthy but light and will benefit from the slight sweetness of this beer style. Try Allagash Brewing's White Beer (5% ABV). The slightly sour coriander and orange peel nose will accentuate the slightly pungent onion. The tangy, slightly bitter taste will contrast with the sweetness of the scallop and earthy oil. This beer style's cloudy appearance is beautiful for a celebration dinner presented in a champagne glass.

Oysters are a shellfish. This pairing will be most successful if fresh oysters and fresh ginger are used. Fresh ginger should have skin that is tender like a leaf, not dry like a brown paper bag. It should be soft enough to scrape the skin off with a spoon. Fresh oysters will smell briny like the sea but never fishy. Their shells should have complexities in the grey tones as opposed to a flat, aged grey. The beauty of cooking oysters on a grill is that they will open on their own. The most difficult part of cooking fresh oysters is opening them without cutting one's hand.

3–5	oysters per person
1	tablespoon fresh ginger
½	grapefruit (for zest and juice)
3	shallots, sliced
	Pinch sugar
1	stick butter
	Splash extra-virgin olive oil
1	bunch chives, chopped
	Pinch salt

Plan for 3 to 5 oysters per person. Create a compound butter of fresh ginger, grapefruit, shallots, butter, chives, and salt. Slice shallots and sauté in a splash of olive oil until translucent over medium heat. Meanwhile, remove skin from ginger with a spoon and add the 1 tablespoon of finely diced ginger to the shallots. Stir over low heat another 1–2 minutes until fragrant. Add the grapefruit juice and zest and sugar and turn off heat. Place mixture in a bowl in the freezer for 3 minutes to cool off. Add butter, fresh chopped chives, and cooled mixture to a food processor and pulse until mixed. Spread out onto waxed paper and form into a log. Put log into freezer for 3 minutes.

Place oysters on hot grill, flat side down. Close lid and cook for about 5 minutes until shells open. Holding the oyster with an oven mitt, remove the top shell and loosen oyster meat from shell with a flick from a small paring knife. Retain as much of the juice in the oyster as possible. The juice is called the liquor and offers a sweet sip to swallow with the oyster meat. Top oysters with a slice of butter and grill until melted, about 1 more minute. Remove, cool for a minute or two, and serve.

Beer Pairing

There are two distinct strategies to pair this dish with beer. Use either session ale with a fragrant spicy nose or a balanced hoppy IPA. Sah'tea is a session ale from Dogfish Head Brewing (9% ABV/6 IBU). This beer is made with a German yeast causing a big mouthfeel and spices including cardamom, ginger, black tea, cinnamon, and black pepper. Session ales are named "session" because they are mild enough to drink several in a session. However, while this brew is light and drinkable, it offers enough spice complexity to stand up to the bitter grapefruit and smoky grill taste. Also from Dogfish Head, the 90 minute IPA (9% ABV/90 IBU) is a very high-hopped but balanced IPA. This IPA is dominated by caramel notes rather than citric or herbal flavors. During the boil, the brew is constantly hopped for a full 90 minutes, leading to a refined, multitonal flavor. Offer both in a pint glass.

BLACK VALENTINE HEIRLOOM BEAN CHILI

B lack valentine beans are a heirloom bean with a thick texture and earthy
flavor. Standard black beans can be used in place of this heirloom bean.

1	cup black valentine beans, dry
2	dried chiles
2	garlic cloves
2	cinnamon sticks
1	teaspoon cumin
1	tablespoon coriander
1	onion, chopped
3	tablespoons honey
	Extra-virgin olive oil, for sauteeing
	Goat cheese or Parmesan (to taste)

Rinse beans under cold, filtered water. Using a colander or strainer works
best. After rinsing, remove beans from water and let dry. Dispose of water.

Meanwhile, add dried chiles to cold, filtered water in a heavy-bottomed pan and bring to a boil. Plan for 1 cup of water per cup of dry
beans, 2 dry chiles per cup of water, and ½ cup dry beans per person.
Once the water boils, turn off the heat and cover for about 30 minutes.
This is infusing the water with chiles.

Uncover the chile water, remove the chiles and add the beans. Pour in
enough dark beer to come at least 1 inch above the beans. Bring to a boil
and add smashed garlic, cinnamon, cumin, and coriander.

Simmer the beans until cooked, about an hour. Stir every 15–20 minutes while simmering and add more beer every time the liquid dips below the top of the beans. When beans are cooked, separate the liquid from the beans by straining the cooked beans into another large pot. Add honey to the bean liquid. Allow the sauce to reduce by at least half over medium heat.

Sauté white onion in olive oil over medium-high heat. Add a pinch of cumin and salt. Add onions to the cooked beans and salt to taste. Pour the reduced bean-honey mixture onto the beans. Add goat cheese or Parmesan while warm. Serve warm or room temperature.

Beer Pairing

Chili offers the perfect opportunity to pair a porter. Deschutes Brewing's Black Butte Porter (5.2% ABV/30 IBU) mimics the chili with a dark, viscous appearance. Similar to the sweet and spicy layers of chili, the porter gleams from black to ruby and offers a mix of sweet malts and a hoppy finish. Offer in pint glass.

SOUTHERN-STYLE GREENS WITH CORNBREAD

℘

S outhern-style greens are traditionally tough collard greens, slow cooked with acids and fats, usually vinegars and pork. To tenderize the greens in this recipe, they are cooked with spicy dill pickle juice.

GREENS

1	bunch collard greens
2	tablespoons olive oil
½	cup pickle juice
1	teaspoon allspice

CORNBREAD

1	cup cornmeal
½	cup flour
2	teaspoons sugar
1	pinch baking soda
1	pinch baking powder
1	cup buttermilk
⅓	cup cream
1	egg
1	cup corn kernels
	Black pepper, to taste

Chop greens into 1-inch squares and remove stems. Use collard greens, chard, or beet greens. Warm a sauté pan over medium-high heat. Add enough olive oil to barely coat the bottom of the pan. Sauté the greens, flipping them in the pan until wilted and vibrantly colored. Add pickle juice and a pinch of salt. Cover, turn to low, and let cook undisturbed for 10 minutes. Uncover, add freshly ground pepper and 1 teaspoon of allspice. Allow to cook until liquid is evaporated. Taste. If still bitter, add more acid, either in the form of citrus juice or stewed tomatoes, recover and cook covered for another 5–10 minutes.

To make cornbread, preheat the oven to 500 degrees with a cast iron skillet inside. Mix cornmeal, flour, sugar, baking soda, and baking powder in a bowl. In another bowl, combine buttermilk, cream, and 1 egg. Whisk until combined. Add the dry ingredients into the wet ingredients and add melted butter and corn kernels. Turn the oven down to 375 degrees, fill the skillet with the cornbread mixture, and bake until a toothpick inserted in the middle comes out clean, about 20 minutes.

Beer Pairing

Pair the vinegar-flavored greens and sweet cakey cornbread with a palate-cleansing slightly sour Lambic. New Belgiun Brewing's Frambozen (6.5% ABV/15.5 IBU) is a sour wheat Lambic made with wild yeast, unmalted wheat, and real raspberries. This and similarly styled brews offer slightly sour fruit flavors like rhubarb, raspberries, and wild strawberries that refresh the tongue by contrasting the cakey texture of the cornbread and offer sweetness to the dry nutmeg and sour vinegar in the greens. Offer in a tulip glass.

EMILY'S GRANDMA'S MAC AND CHEESE

This recipe for macaroni and cheese is layered and baked. Many recipes call for a warm cheese sauce poured over macaroni noodles. Either approach will work for the beer pairing as long as very sharp cheddar cheese is used.

3	cups macaroni
1½	cups extra-sharp cheddar, grated
1	white onion, chopped
2	cloves garlic, minced
2	tablespoons butter/olive oil
12	ounces sour cream
⅓	cup whole milk
	Pinch salt
	Black pepper, to taste

Preheat the oven to 350 degrees. Bring water to a boil in a pasta pot, and add a pinch of salt. Add 3 cups of macaroni noodles and cook until al dente.

While the noodles cook, sauté onion over medium heat until translucent in butter and olive oil. Add garlic and sauté for 2 more minutes. Remove from the heat, place in a mixing bowl, and add sour cream and cheddar cheese. Mix the sour cream, onion, garlic, and cheese in a large mixing bowl until it forms a paste.

Layer cooked noodles in a thin layer along the bottom of a deep baking pan. Add a layer of paste to cover the noodles. Add noodles, then paste, repeating until the dish is filled to the top. Be sure the final layer is paste. Pour milk over the top and finish with freshly ground pepper.

Bake until top is crunchy and inside is melted, about 40 minutes. Serve with hot sauce.

Beer Pairing

Pair this dish with a high-hop Imperial IPA to stand up to the sharp cheddar and high dairy content. Russian River Brewing's Pliny the Elder Imperial IPA (8% ABV/100 IBU) is an excellent example of this style. With a softly sweet malted caramel background, the beer opens up to a very pronounced hop flavor. Rather than a bold rosemary or citric taste as found in an American Pale Ale, this beer is balanced and bold like the macaroni, showcasing strong flavors in harmony. Expect this pairing to convert red wine drinkers to beer fans. Serve in a small pint glass.

FRIED CHICKEN AND BEER SYRUP

Use a whole free-range, antibiotic-free chicken for this recipe. The chicken will be much less expensive if purchased whole.

1	whole chicken
1	cup buttermilk
2	cups all-purpose flour
⅛	cup salt
⅛	cup pepper
1	tablespoon paprika
	Crisco
2	white onions
1	bottle flat beer
1	cup brown sugar
1	teaspoon vanilla extract

Brine the entire chicken in buttermilk for 24 hours. To cut the chicken, place it on a cutting board breast side up, legs pointing toward the cutter. Run a small knife between the area where the leg and thigh attach to the breast to open the skin between the legs and the body. Once the skin has been removed, place an open palm under the leg and pull against the socket until the bone pops from the joint. Use the knife to carve any remaining meat and separate the leg from the body. Place the leg and thigh skin side down and cut along the line of fat to separate the leg from the thigh. Return to the chicken; cut along either side of the breast bone—the bone that divides the two chicken breasts. This will separate the breasts from the carcass. Allow the breast bone and the rib cage to guide the knife. Use small strokes and cut the breast away from these bones at an angle. At the top of the chicken where the neck was is the wish bone. Use this bone as a guide as well to cut away from when removing the breast. Flip the skin of the breast down and cut along the joint between the wing and breast to remove the wing. Retain the carcass to make soup or stock.

Per one chicken, mix the ratio listed of salt, pepper, and tablespoon of paprika with flour in a bowl. Dip the chicken pieces into the dry mixture, coating all sides. Lift the chicken above the bowl, shake the excess off, and dip again. Rest on a plate and repeat with the rest of the chicken. In a cast iron skillet, heat vegetable oil or Crisco over high heat until shimmering at 350 degrees. Preheat the oven to 375 degrees. Add onions that have been peeled and quartered into the oil. As the chicken fries, the onion will flavor the oil.

Place the chicken into the frying pan and cook until the internal temperature is 140 degrees, about 5 minutes per side. Place on a wire rack in the oven and bake until 160 degrees. Offer beer syrup for dipping.

For the syrup, combine a bottle of flat stout beer with 1 cup brown sugar and 1 teaspoon vanilla extract. Set in a pan over medium-high heat and bring to a boil. Watch to be sure the mixture does not boil over. Turn down to medium and continue to watch. No need to stir. Allow mixture to reduce to about 1 cup.

(continued)

Beer Pairing

Pair this meal with an Oatmeal Stout. Firestone Walker Brewing's Velvet Merlin (5.5% ABV/30 IBU) offers a level of complexity to the stout syrup by providing a bready, vanilla taste that almost acts as the waffle often offered with fried chicken. The oily and crispy chicken shines as the beer is soft, creamy and mild. Despite the mild brew flavor, the presence of an oat texture on the tongue ensures that the beer does not disappear into the dish.

LAMB BONE STEW

This recipe is based on a Moroccan approach to cooking where cubed meat is placed in a large, glazed pottery dish called a tagine.

1   pound lamb
1   tablespoon ginger
1   tablespoon coriander seeds
1   tablespoon red pepper
1   tablespoon saffron
1   tablespoon salt
3   small red onion
4   cloves garlic
2   tablespoons olive oil
1   cup beer
2   cinnamon sticks
1   citrus
1   cup dried fruit: mixture of dates, apricots, raisins, figs, and prunes
4   tablespoons honey
    Garnish: almond, parsley, cilantro

Gather a pound of shoulder or leg lamb meat and ensure that the farmer or butcher provides the bones as well. Dice the meat into similar-shaped 1-inch cubes using a sharp knife so as not to tear the meat. Reserve the

(continued)

bones. In a dry small skillet, toast the ginger, coriander seeds, red pepper, saffron, and salt. Toasting dried spices reactivates their oils. Toast over low heat just until the kitchen smells of ginger, most likely in less than 3 minutes.

Chop onions and garlic and sauté in olive oil in a large skillet until wilted and fragrant. Add the meat, paired beer, cinnamon sticks, and the toasted spices. Fill the pan with water until all meat is submerged and cover with a lid. Bring the meat to a mild simmer and maintain at that level for 1 hour. Boiling the liquid will make the meat tough, so remain at a mild simmer. While the meat simmers, zest a citrus: orange, tangerine, or pomello will all work. As an hour slowly passes, add a bit more water if needed to the lamb to keep it simmering. After 1 hour, add the citrus zest and a pile of dried fall fruit into the pan with more water if needed. Dates, apricots, raisins, figs, and prunes will work. Simmer for 5 minutes. Remove the meat from the pan and add honey and the lamb bones. Cook the bones on high, turning until browned on all sides. Remove the bones, return the meat to the pan, and serve with chopped almonds, chopped parsley, and cilantro.

Beer Pairing

Pair lamb bone stew with a Belgian-style Pale Ale. This style of beer tends to have a floral nose and a spicy taste, similar to the lamb. While the lamb will have a gamey brined finish that weighs heavily on the tongue and jowls, the beer will finish lightly on the front of the tongue with bright hops that go up the nose. The Lost Abbey Brewing's Devotion Belgian-style Pale Ale (6.25% ABV) offers a nose of dried apricot that mimics the dried fruit in the dish, the light sting of pear on the front of the tongue that balances out the brined flavor, and a spicy mouthfeel with clove and black pepper that complements the red pepper and saffron. The hop finish highlights the slow-roasted, caramelized garlic and onion. Serve in a pint glass.

NEW YEAR'S BEER AND CAVIAR PAIRING

aviar traditionally refers to wild harvested sturgeon fish eggs. Sustainably farmed sturgeon caviar can be equally flavorful. Caviar must be kept chilled and eaten as soon as opened on a mother of pearl spoon. The flavor can be easily tainted when kept open too long or interacting with metal. Quality caviar will hold small egg shapes as it is removed from the tin and melt into the tongue like a savory, umami, smooth butter. Traditional garnish includes crème fraîche and a small blini pastry.

Beer Pairing

Pair fresh sturgeon caviar with a light, citric, wheat beer that has a dry finish. Consider pairing with individual pulp segments of very cold mandarin oranges, a wheat blini, and crème fraîche.

Drink Firestone Walker Brewing's Solace (4.8% ABV/15 IBU) in a tulip glass. This unfiltered ale is actually produced during the summer but if purchased in late August, early September, can store well until New Year's Eve. Expect this pairing to produce flavors of umami, orange, salt, and fruits. For a sharper pairing, drink a creamy, unfiltered "Biére Brut." This crossover-style ale is often cave aged and similar in flavor to dry champagne.

Drink Boston Beer's Infinium (10.3%/9 IBU) in a flute. This is a crisp champagne-like beer with sharp bubbles and a big aroma. The crisp malt character and delicate fruit notes contain a slight citrus feel. It is bottle conditioned, meaning that it does not have to be fresh right from the store. It changes with age. Expect this pairing to produce flavors of umami, tarragon, cream, chestnut, and salt.

ROSEWATER PAVLOVA

Pavlova is a light, sugary sweet. In this recipe, floral rosewater links this dessert to boozy barleywine. Other flower waters or extracts can be used in place of the rosewater.

4	egg whites
1½	cups sugar
2	teaspoons cornstarch
½	teaspoon white vinegar
½	teaspoon vanilla
2	tablespoons rosewater or flower water or 1 teaspoon extract
	Pinch salt

Preheat oven to 225 degrees. Place egg whites with salt in a bowl and whisk with a hand mixer until billowy, about 3 minutes on high speed. While whisking, slowly add sugar and then cornstarch. The mixture will form stiff, glossy peaks within 5 minutes. Use a spatula to fold in vinegar, vanilla, and rosewater.

Spray a muffin pan with nonstick spray. Drop spoonfuls of pavlova mixture into each muffin hole. Bake until the crust is pale and golden, 40 minutes to 1 hour. Turn the oven off and let cool inside for at least 1 hour or up to 12 hours.

(continued)

Beer Pairing

Pair these floral meringues with a high-sugar barleywine. Try Uinta Brewing's Cockeyed Cooper (11% ABV/65 IBU) in a snifter. This pairing will create a vanilla nose in both the food and the beer. The beer will offer flavors of smooth brown sugar that will complement the white, crumbly sugar texture of the meringue. This pairing will trick the tongue into finding raisin and oak flavors and a palate-staining light plum.

LAVENDER-HOPPED PANNA COTTA

Just as hops are added to beer to provide flavor, lavender is added to the cream to flavor the panna cotta.

- ½ cup filtered water
- 2 teaspoons unflavored gelatin
- 1½ cups sour cream
- 3 tablespoons Meyer lemon
- 1 teaspoon vanilla
- 1½ cups heavy whipping cream
- ½ cup raw cane sugar
- 2 tablespoons lavender

Combine water with gelatin in a small bowl for about 20 minutes until softened. In a larger bowl, combine sour cream, lemon juice, and vanilla. Meyer lemon offers a sweeter juice than a traditional lemon. In a small saucepan, combine whipping cream and sugar. "Hop" the cream by adding lavender in a small saucepan, bring it to just below a boil (look for bubbles popping on the surface), and stir to dissolve the sugar. Take it off the heat, cover it, and let it sit for 10 minutes. Strain out the lavender. Mix the gelatin and water into the hot cream. Stir to dissolve. Whisk in sour cream mixture until mixed. Pour the mixture into a measuring cup with a spout, and then pour into ramekins. Cover and chill for at least 4 hours. Panna cottas can be served any time between 4 hours and 24 hours, and then they begin to fall apart.

(*continued*)

Beer Pairing

A Belgian-style double or a strong ale highlights the herbal creaminess in this dish. Russian River's Damnation Belgian-style double (7.75% ABV/25 IBU) is golden in color, which can be deceitful. This beer is balanced but strong. The banana nose on the beer and the almond, cherry, lavender nose on the dessert blend well and create a fruity, floral experience. The beer finishes with a dry lasting twinge, contrasting the light creaminess of the panna cotta. Serve in a tulip glass.

CHAPTER 7

Hosting a Beer and Cheese Pairing Party

This final chapter provides detailed tasting notes to pair fifteen beer styles with cheese. Each pairing includes suggestions for charcuterie, accoutrements, and glassware selection. Cheese does not pair with "beer" categorically. Rather each style of beer offers pairings in and of itself, just as each style of wine and spirits offers diversity and complexity in their cheese pairings.

The Basics for a Tasting Party

As a tasting party, plan that each guest will be provided a 3- to 4-ounce taste of each beer and that four to eight beers will be featured. One 12-oz beer will offer three tastes and a 22-oz bottle will offer six tastes. Also, consider providing a low-alcohol session beer that guests can enjoy in larger quantities. Be cautious if this ratio is followed; each guest has the potential to drink the equivalent of several bottles of beer. Make responsible choices and designate a driver for all participants. In some states, party hosts can be held responsible should an accident occur on the road after providing alcohol to guests.

In selecting pairings, consider diversity for your guests. Some beer pairing guides suggest that if the audience is new to beer, focus on lighter low-hop brews, and if the audience is experienced in beer, burn their taste buds off with hops and alcohol. We disagree. Perhaps the reason some have avoided beer as their beverage of choice is not because they avoid flavor, but because they may be drinkers of bourbon and cabernet. It may be because they prefer flavor and have only experienced low-quality brews. These tasting guests may appreciate a high-hopped IPA paired perfectly with bold smoked cheddar to experience the same level of intense complexities offered in their other drinks. Experienced beer drinkers will seek high-quality, adventurous beers be they light pilsners or big IPAs. These beer connoisseurs may appreciate a lighter pairing that highlights the delicate flavors of a mild brew and silky cheese. After purchasing, remember to store your brews in the warmer section of the fridge away from light. The door is an ideal spot.

Provide a pitcher of fresh cool water to pour into glassware between tastes and a dump bucket to pour out rinse water. Provide a separate glass of water for your guests to stay hydrated between tastes. Consider providing a printed menu of beers and cheeses being paired with room for guests to make notes. Alternatively, consider a blind tasting in which the beer bottles remain covered in numbered bags. This allows guests to comment only on flavor and cheese pairing without influence from the beer name or brand. Remember to refer to chapter 1 on artfully pairing beer, to select and prepare glassware, and to guide guests on how to find flavors in the brews and cheeses.

Suggested Pairings

This section contains a list of fifteen styles of beer with suggested cheese and charcuterie pairings. Each brew varies in characteristic. If four to eight of the listed items were selected and then executed in the order listed, the pairing experience should be successful.

Pilsner/Kölsch: The crisp mouthfeel, high effervescence, briny taste, and smell of nutmeg pair well with delicate, tangy cheeses and mild, citric, and fishy charcuterie. Consider pairing a soft goat chèrve, mild cured salmon with lemon zest, and the green tomatillo/tomato jam from the Spring chapter. The French Fleur Verte is perfect for this pairing. It is goat's milk cheese coated in pink peppercorns, thyme, and tarragon. Alternate cheeses to consider are the Mexican Cotija cheese, which is hard, salty, and crumbly or a high-quality Parmesan. Offer peppered water crackers as well. This pairing will produce flavors of nutmeg, lemon, thyme, and the pectin found in green apples. Offer a champagne flute or footed pilsner glass with this beer.

Blonde: Often referred to as a beach beer, blonde ales have a soft, rhythmic "bobbing in the waves" mouthfeel, mild tropical fruit fragrance, and a flavor of oatmeal and grains that pair well with crisp textures and mild fruits. Consider pairing a salsa of diced peach, jicama, and cilantro on a cheese crisp with a sharp, aged Italian provolone or a soft, slightly melted camembert. This pairing will produce light, approachable flavors of citrus, toasted coriander, pineapple, and straw. Offer a pint glass with this beer.

Witbier /Wheat: Cloudy in appearance, slightly thick in mouthfeel with a nasal drinking experience, wheat or witbier pairs well with silky, slightly sweet soft cheeses that balance out the slightly sour brew. Floral feta cheeses in oil or soft dilled havarti, with toasted sweet macadamia nuts, and light tangy cured meats like smoked trout served on pear slices create a beautiful cheese plate. This pairing will produce flavors of grass, banana, celery, and resin. Offer a figure-eight-shaped glass or weiss glass with this beer.

Saison/Farmhouse: Floral, musty and complex in smell and taste, Saison reeks of the farmhouse brewing, and as such, holds up to soft, ripe cheeses. Consider joining these pungent flavors on a skewer: a vinegary French cornichon pickle, the pickled radishes mentioned in the Spring chapter of this book, an interesting green olive, a grilled anchovy, and a soft washed cheese such as Mt. Tam smeared on top. Alternatively a light pâté of poultry or pork on a buttery cracker with an alcohol-soaked Taleggio or drunken goat cheese would be excellent here. Do not be tempted to use a Brie cheese; the high fat and creamy taste will not highlight the complexities of the beer. Lobby your local cheese shop or grocery for something stinky with an edible rind, such as an Epoisses from central France. This pairing will provide flavors of wet straw, blooming or decaying flowers, and the earth after a rain. Offer a tulip glass with this brew.

Amber/Red Ale: With a red, slightly transparent appearance, and soft, roasty texture with a slight presence of hops, pair these ales with onion and mustard flavors. Serve alongside soft Irish-pub-style cheeses, cut into cubes, such as mild cheddars filled with green onions or jack cheeses with mustard seeds alongside grilled poultry sausages with sage. Because this beer is soft in texture, squeeze the cheeses slightly when purchasing to ensure that they are also soft in texture. This pairing will produce flavors of mild onion, corn, light caramel, and slight syrup. Offer a pint glass or a mug with this brew.

Brown Ale: Brown in appearance, syrupy in texture, floral in flavor, and mild in mouthfeel, pair these ales with cheeses that are high in cream, smooth in body, and accented with charcuterie that is floral and grilled. Pairing the color of the beer with browns and purples in produce and cheese will highlight the robust color of the brew. Consider a beautiful plate of grilled Brie topped with fresh figs, crispy Mexican chorizo, and a smear of pumpkin or apple butter on pumpernickel. Alternatively, small flatbreads with an herbal Spanish sheep's milk manchego, rosemary, and chestnuts would be wonderful as well. This pairing will produce flavors of honey, rose petals, balsamic vinegar, and vanilla and will also go well with sweet potato chips. Offer a mug or pint glass with this brew.

Pale Ale: Pale ales begin the presence of highly detectable hops in the beer lineup. With a stinging mouthfeel, piney or citric nose, and deceptive yellow appearance, pair these ales with aged, sharp, or very buttery cheeses. Consider the raw red onion and mango salad presented in the Summer chapter or offer a pesto of sundried tomatoes and pine nuts. Either charcuterie option would pair wonderfully with fresh, creamy burrata mozzarella or fresh, whole-milk ricotta. This pairing will produce flavors of pine, citrus, acid, and butter. Offer a pint glass or tulip glass with this pairing.

India Pale Ale (IPA): With a hoppy nose, spicy flavor, and high alcohol presence, IPA offer the opportunity to pair high spice, high oil, and offensively sharp cheeses. Consider using the North African bell pepper sauce harissa on sharp cheddar with kale chips or treat guests to the ideal Italian cheese board with chewy ciabatta bread, rows of spiced bresaola under acidic green olive oil, fennel-orange scented olives, and Parmesan aged until nearly rotten. This pairing will produce sharp flavors of citrus, spice, and wood. Offer a pint glass with this brew.

Imperial IPA: With a smoky, hoppy nose, complex spicy flavor, and even higher alcohol presence, Imperial IPAs pair with peppered meats and dry, salty cheeses. The ideal cheese plate to pair with an Imperial IPA would be small sandwiches of smoked pastrami, with a spread of chilled beet horseradish or rhubard jam on brown bread offered alongside shavings of salty pecorino romano or ricotta salata. This pairing will produce flavors of cigar, pepper, smoke, and cedar wood. Offer a snifter glass with this brew.

Stout: Lingering on the palette, obsidian in color, and pure chocolate on the nose, stout offers the opportunity to pair with an unapologetically sweet cheese plate. Offer a dense brownie or chocolate cookie, the lemon confit from the Spring chapter, fresh raspberries, and a fondue of warmed honeyed ricotta or mascarpone that has been whipped. This pairing will produce flavors of chocolate, licorice, cream, and earth. Offer an Imperial pint glass with this brew.

Porter: Midnight in color, roasty in flavor, and soft but full in mouthfeel, porters offer an exciting opportunity to consider a pairing plate that mimics the complexities of a mole sauce. Offer bittersweet chocolate, smoked duck, dried coconut, and smoked aged cheddar or, if Oktoberfest looms, enjoy the Fall chapter's smoked Gouda sauce with salty, doughy pretzels. If truffles fit your epicurean style, offer cubes of crispy pancetta, truffled cheese, and lavender honey on pumpernickel. This pairing will offer flavors of coffee, gaminess, earthiness, and cinnamon. Offer an Imperial pint glass with this brew.

Barleywine: With a highly viscous mouthfeel, nose of aged and dried fruit and herbs, and flavors of brandy, barleywines must be paired with aged cheeses and overripe fruits. Join the Bacon Jam from the Fall chapter, candied pecans, and a penicillin-heavy blue cheese or a gorgonzola dulce on soft, doughy olive or rosemary bread. Expect flavors of raisin, alcohol, jasmine, and molasses in this pairing. Offer a goblet or red wine glass with this brew.

Strong Ale: Strong ales are usually categorized as golden or dark. Golden strong ales have a nose of apples and pear with a beautiful lacey head. Pair with hunks of honeycomb, raw walnuts, sliced red apples, and an aged Colby cheese. Dark strong ales have a nose of cherries and a malty, soft texture. Pair with thin slices of gamey meats like venison, topped with cherries in brandy or cranberry sauce, dried ginger, and slices of a mineral-rich cheese like a Spanish valdeon. Offer a snifter with both types of strong ale.

Sour: The bold, sour characteristics of a sour ale allow for salted, fishy, and acidic flavors in cheese and charcuterie pairing. Prepare a plate of salt cod soaked in lime juice and a seeded baguette to pair with sharp shaved pecorino romano. Alternatively, if the beer is incredibly sour and sharp, consider topping the pecorino with cashews and a sweet and smoky fruit jam. Flavors in this pairing will include savory, pungent, drying, and nutty. Offer a tulip glass with this brew.

Fruit Lambic: Fruit Lambics vary in the specific fruit flavor they carry but offer high champagne-like effervescence, biting mouthfeel, and soft, slightly sour flavors that hit the front of the tongue. To highlight the fruit flavors, consider a dried fruit Stilton and enjoy a crumbly texture that plays off the effervescence, or consider a sharp aged white cheddar similar to the grilled peach recipe discussed in the Summer chapter. Smoked almonds and toasted rye bread offer a grounding counterbalance flavor to the sour fruit. This pairing will produce sour, fruity, floral, drying, and stinging flavors. Offer a flute or champagne glass with this pairing.

The Party

Right before guests arrive, bring the beers out of the refrigerator. Put the pilsners, saisons, and pale ales on ice to maintain a 35- to 45-degree serving temperature. Unless the outside temperature is very high, allow the IPAs, porters and barleywines to rest on the counter until they reach 45 to 55 degrees.

Allow the cheeses the same opportunity to open up at proper temperature as the beers. Warm the cheeses at room temperature before the party. Each cheese has a maximum of 2 hours to linger at temperatures between 40 and 140 without health risk, according to food industry standards. Present each cheese and accompaniments on their own platters with serving utensils. Consider placing a small table tent on each platter with the name or number of the paired brew so that guests do not help themselves to the incorrect pairing.

Guide your guests' tasting experience. Kick off with a demonstration to pour beer as described in chapter 1, right into the glass. Then, hold the glass up to the light and describe the visual details in familiar terms that they can relate to: cloudy or clear, carbonated or flat, yellow or red or brown or black, thin or thick. Next, swirl and smell the beer, describing your experience in familiar terms as well: nutty, grainy, sweet, boozy, sour, citric, herbal, spicy, or roasty. Finally, taste the beer and taste the cheese. Discuss the mouthfeel and flavor. In regard to mouthfeel, consider whether the beer is biting or soft and thick or thin. How does the beer change with the cheese? Does it become thinner or thicker? Do new flavors emerge in the brew once the cheese is on the tongue too? In regard to flavor, consider printing the flavor wheel and distributing it to your guests as a tool to increase their flavor vocabulary. Educate guests on the knowledge gained in the introduction of this book. Do not mimic wine tasting and spit the wine out. Remember that beer must be swallowed for full flavor enjoyment.

Enjoy the party! Not all guests will enjoy all pairings and all brews. The role of the host or hostess of a beer and cheese pairing is not to throw a tea party filled with niceties. The role is to create opportunities for good discussion, develop an appreciation for fine brews, and ensure all guests arrive home safely. Cheers!

Glossary

ABV—Alcohol by volume (ABV) is measured by percentage, representing the amount of alcohol contained in a liquid beverage. For example, 5% ABV means that 5% of 100% of a beer is alcohol.

Alcohol content—amount of alcohol contained within a liquid beverage, represented by ABV.

Ale—beer that is brewed at a warm temperature.

Amber—ale beer that is the color of amber and has sweet and smoky flavors because as more roasted amber malts enter the sweet wort boil, the sweet flavors shine through without being overshadowed by spicy hops.

Barleywine—has a dried fruit flavor and high-alcohol content because more sugars, referred to as higher gravity, are used in the fermentation process. This brings the alcohol content to almost that of a wine, hence the name.

Barrel aged—rather than bottle or keg beer right after it is brewed, the beer ages in a barrel such as one made from oak, to develop more flavors.

Belgian style—Belgian-style beers are brewed with more than the four basic ingredients—water, yeast, malts, and hops—found in German-style brewing. These could include berries, pine needles, herbs, and other organic flavor agents. These beers tend to have complex flavors.

Berliner Weiss—German beer that is unfiltered making it cloudy with a slightly sour, light lemon flavor.

Bitterness Units—measure of the amount of hops in a beer from 0 to several hundred.

Blonde—ale with light, bready flavors because high levels and a wide variety of pale malts are used in brewing.

Botulism—disease that can be food borne from improper preservation.

Brisket—cut of meat from the chest of a cow.

Brown—cinnamon-color ale with mild, nuttier flavors. Darker malts and almost no hops are used in brewing.

Carbonation—bubbles; in beer, carbonation is caused by yeast.

Chamomile—soothing, mild tea made from plant.

Chimichurri—Argentinean steak sauce made of herbs, oil, and vinegar.

Clarity—how transparent a liquid is.

Crema—Hispanic dairy product similar to a sour cream or a crème fraîche.

Dry—leaves the tongue clear, refreshed, and uncoated.

Effervescence—amount of carbonation in the beer and the size of the bubbles.

Farmhouse style—open-fermented with floral, slightly sour flavors.

Head—amount of white foam at the top of the beer. If a beer has no head, it is flat or in a dirty glass.

Hibiscus—flower often used as a dry ingredient.

Hoppy/hops—"salt and pepper" of beer; flowers from the hop vines are a natural preservative and add flavor to the sweet wort.

IBUs—International bitterness units; measure of the amount of hops in a beer from 0 to several hundred.

India Pale Ale (IPA)/Imperial IPA—ale that has high levels of bitter and citric spice because a large amount of diverse hops is used.

Lager—beer brewed and stored at cold temperatures.

Lambic—open-fermented ale that attracts the floral flavors of wild yeast and has sour fruit flavors and high carbonation.

Malt—cooked grains that create sweet wort. Toasting malts leads to a darker color in beer.

Meilgaard Beer Flavor Wheel—developed in the 1970s by scientist Morton Meilgaard as a tool to identify flavors in beer.

Mouthfeel—texture of liquid in the mouth from thick-like syrup to thin like water.

Nutella—Italian brand of hazelnut chocolate spread with the same texture as a smooth peanut butter.

Organic—pesticide-free.

Pale Ale—has balance of sweetness, light body, and spice because lighter malts and a high level of hops are used.

Phenolic—taste or smell like a rubbery Band-Aid.

Pickling salt—salt used for pickling because it dissolves in liquid without caking.

Pilsner—lager with light, crisp, hopped flavors and high effervescence because it is brewed at colder temperatures, cold fermented, medium hopped, filtered, and then stored to temper the hops.

Porter—ale with a syrup flavor because a combination of sweet amber and chocolate malts are used to create a sweet, dark, full liquid.

Saison—open-fermented Belgian-style ale with fruity, tart, and sour flavors because it gathers the wild yeast around the fermentation tank.

Session Ale—low ABV beer that is light enough in flavor to enjoy multiple servings of the same brew in a drinking "session."

Snifter—short, bulbous glass used for brandy and barleywine.

Stout—ale with dry coffee flavor and medium body because the black malts have been roasted to a dark, almost black color and few hops are added.

Strong—mostly open-fermented ale with flavors of complex fruit and soft texture with high-alcohol content.

Umami—one of the five flavors in addition to sweet, salty, sour, and savory. Umami is meaty and savory and is found in mushrooms and duck.

Viscosity—thickness of the beer.

Witbier/Weissbier/Wheat—unfiltered ale with a thick, creamy flavor of wheat because wheat is the predominant grain used in brewing.

Wort—liquid created from mashing brewed grains.

Yeast—live cultures that ferment to create alcohol in beer.

Bibliography

Guggiana, Marissa. *Primal Cuts: Cooking with America's Best Butchers.* New York: Welcome Books, 2010.

Michelson, Patricia. *Cheese: Exploring Taste and Tradition.* Layton, UT: Gibbs Smith, 2010.

Oliver, Garret. *The Oxford Companion to Beer.* New York: Oxford University Press, 2011.

Ruhlman, Michael, and Brian Polcyn. *Charcuterie: The Craft of Salting, Smoking, and Curing.* New York: W.W. Norton & Company, 2005.

Ziedrich, Linda. *The Joy of Pickling.* Boston, MA: The Harvard Common Press, 2009.

Index

Lobster and Homemade Butter,
71–73
Lost Abbey Brewing: Carnivale, 27;
Devotion Belgian-style Pale Ale,
127
Lost Coast Brewing's Downtown
Brown, 34, 50
Lucky 13 (Lagunitas Brewing
Company), 37

Mac and Cheese, Emily's Grandma's,
120–21
Maibock, 20; Gordon Biersch
Brewing's Maibock, 24; Rogue
Ales' Dead Guy Ale, 24
malts, 142; in brewing process, 15;
cacao and, 27
Mammoth Brewing: Golden Trout
Pilsner, 31; Nut Brown, 27
Mango Caprese with Homemade
Mozzarella, 59–61
Märzens, 79, 83
meat, selecting, 7–8. *See also specific
meat*
Meilgaard Beer Flavor Wheel, 12, 142
Mendocino Imperial Barleywine-style
Ale, 107
Le Merle Belgian Style (North Coast
Brewing Company), 70
Meyer Lemon Curd, 48–49
Monterey Bay Aquarium's Seafood
Watch List, 8, 35
mouthfeel, 143

mustard or tomalley, crab, 36–37;
Mustard Sauce, 39

New Belgium Brewing: Blue Paddle
Pilsner, 24; Fat Tire Amber Ale,
37, 105; Frambozen, 119; Red
Hoptober, 94
New Year's beer and caviar pairing,
128
nitrates, 41–42
North Coast Brewing Company:
Acme Pale Ale, 27, 38; Brother
Thelonious, 27; Le Merle
Belgian Style Farmhouse Ale, 70;
Scrimshaw Pilsner, 31, 58
Nut Brown (Mammoth Brewing), 27
Nutella, 143

Odyssey (Allagash Brewing), 75
oils, 8–9
Oktoberfest (Pyramid Brewery), 94
Oktoberfest Kraut and Sausage,
95–96
Oktoberfest lager (Boston Beer), 96
Oktoberfest Pretzels and Smoked
Gouda Sauce, 93–94
olive oil, 8–9
onions: Corned Beef, Green Onion
Champ, and Cabbage, 40–43;
Scallops with Caramelized Leeks,
111–13
open fermentation, 15. *See also*
Lambics; strong ales

Walker Brewing's Velvet Merlin
Oatmeal Stout, 77, 124
warm fermentation, 16
water: in brewing process, 15; for
tasting party, 134
wheat beers: Allagash Brewing's
Odyssey, 75; Anchor Brewing's
Summer Wheat, 68; Boston Beer's
Cherry Wheat, 103; The Bruery's
Hottenroth Berliner Weiss, 103;
Hefeweizen, 53; temperature for,
11. *See also* witbier/weissbier/wheat

White Beer (Allagash Brewing), 113
Whole Salt-Roasted Fish, 62–63
Wilco Tango Foxtrot Brown Ale
(Lagunitas Brewing Company),
100
winter beers, 2, 19, 79, 109–10
witbier/weissbier/wheat, 143; beer-
food pairing with, 17, 135
wort, 143; in brewing process, 15

yeast, 143; in brewing process, 15–16;
protection of strains, 7

About the Authors

Emily Baime and Darin Michaels live on the river in Sacramento and run Community Tap and Table. Tap and Table is a mission-oriented business offering hands-on cooking classes, private chef services, beer dinners, culinary trips, and beer-food education with proceeds benefiting area nonprofits.

Emily studied Hospitality and Tourism at San Diego State University and Leadership in Public Policy at the University of Southern California. She is passionate about food policy, active in the Slow Food Movement, and is the general manager of a business alliance. She has lived and worked around the globe, with a special place in her heart for Australia.

Darin has worked for more than nineteen years in sales, marketing, and brewing for Sam Adams and Coors Brewing Co. and represented the beers of Sierra Nevada, Redhook, Russian River, Alaskan, Mendocino, Anchor, Ballast Point, Bear Republic, Deschutes, Dogfish Head, Full Sail, Lagunitas, New Belgium, and many others. Darin has two children, Jake (19) and Macey (16). He attended Washington State University.